10-9-05

Dear Carla,

May the Lord ble

Kenneth McGee

Jude:20

WHAT IS PENTECOST REALLY LIKE?

by
Kenneth R. McGee

Unless otherwise indicated, all Scripture quotations are taken from the Holy Bible, King James Version.

Cover Design by Clint Davis, Boundless Interactive Media

Printed in the United States of America

ISBN 0-9712311-8-4

DEDICATION

TO MY WONDERFUL FAMILY

I want to dedicate this book to people I love. To Gretnia, my wonderful wife of more than forty-six years. She has been by my side, encouraging me every step of the way. Without her love and support I would never have been able to make it. The Lord gave me a perfect helpmate.

To Kenny, my son, who, back in December 2001, urged me to put the materials I have been preaching for the last forty-six years, into a book. I appreciate his encouragement and support. To Kathy, my daughter-in-law, his faithful companion.

To Tammy, my daughter, for her faithful support all down through the years.

To Karmen, Kamber and Kelly, my beautiful and talented grand-daughters.

To Tom Greene, my nephew, who, in December 2001, also urged me to put my thoughts and message on the Holy Ghost into a book.

To Bridgette Tomlin, Tom Greene's daughter, who transcribed my preaching tapes.

I want to express my appreciation to my granddaughter, Karmen, for her help in getting everything on the computer for me.

I also want to thank Lupe Sheppard for her work in helping me arrange the materials.

Without their support, I probably would not have done the book at this time. I must admit, however, I have enjoyed putting all the information down on paper. I pray the book will be a blessing to everyone who reads it.

ACKNOWLEDGEMENTS

There are several people I want to thank for being an inspiration to me in this project. I am sure they may never know that they have been a help to me, but I want to publicly recognize them.

There have been several evangelists down through the years whose preaching on the subject of the Baptism with the Holy Spirit stirred my heart and caused me to search diligently the Scriptures. Their messages influenced me greatly.

Don Brankel is a great Holy Ghost preacher whose ministry has touched my heart. I had him for many revivals during the years I was a pastor.

Warren Litzman was another evangelist who came to Faith Tabernacle a number of times. He is deceased now, but he made a great impact on my life.

Jerry Minton was an evangelist whose ministry on the Holy Spirit greatly impacted my life. I never had the privilege of meeting him, but I listened to a number of his preaching tapes more than twenty years ago.

John G. Hall, a great prophecy preacher, while preaching at Faith Tabernacle, began one of the greatest messages on the Baptism with the Holy Spirit I have ever heard. When he finished we had a tremendous outpouring of the Holy Spirit. That message caused me to use all the Old Testament Scriptures as a reference when I presented my messages on the Holy Spirit.

As a young minister, I was required to read a number of books. One of the books that influenced my ministry on the Holy Spirit was Myer Pearlman's book, "Knowing The Doctrines of the Bible", published in 1937 by Gospel Publishing House. I am indebted to the author of that book for challenging me to study diligently on the subject of the Holy Spirit.

"Strong's Exhaustive Concordance of the Bible", became my source of finding the meaning of every Greek and Hebrew word I used in the book.

TABLE OF CONTENTS

FOREWORD BY ARMON NEWBURN

First, I would like to congratulate the author on a very practical, down to earth book that deals with an extremely important issue confronting the church as well as our personal living — THE BAPTISM IN THE HOLY SPIRIT.
Here, the author couples together personal experiences, events and miracles while emphasizing the necessity of being baptized in the Holy Spirit and speaking in tongues as the initial physical evidence of the baptism in the Holy Spirit (Acts 2:4).

Emphasis is placed on scriptural truth that the baptism in the Holy Spirit is a distinct experience from conversion, which agrees with the scriptures (Acts 8:16, 9:17, 19:2).

As you read this book you will be thrilled by the many revival experiences of the author, clearly revealing that God meets individuals in a variety of ways, yet the end results are the same as individuals follow the scriptural guidelines to repent, be baptized and receive the promise of the baptism in the Holy Spirit (Acts 2:38). Receiving the baptism in the Holy Spirit in New Testament times was a very real and vivid experience for the believer, and the baptism in the Holy Spirit is no less real today.

The author is quick to point out the need for the church to face the challenge of renewal, and teach what the Bible teaches about the baptism in the Holy Spirit in order that we may experience the full potential of Pentecost.

You will find this book challenging, encouraging, and factual as the author pours out his heart, desiring for the church today to experience Pentecost and the promised power.

Armon Newburn
Former District Superintendent and
General Council Executive Presbyter of the Assemblies of God

FOREWORD BY TOM GREENE

My earliest childhood memories include a wealth of experiences in church. From infancy, it was a fact of life that we would be faithful to the house of God. Strong among those early memories was the pulpit manner of a young evangelist who preached in our church frequently. He was a man of God who spoke with a passion and emotion rivaled by few. Noticeably, there was never a message delivered concerning any topic or text that did not include emphasis on the Holy Spirit. It was obvious to me that the strong conviction of this minister was that any believer without "the baptism of the Holy Spirit with the evidence of speaking in other tongues" was short-changing their life and the lives of those they touched.

It was in the fire of one of those revivals that I felt compelled to rush to the altar with a commitment that I would not leave until I had received this gift for myself. It was at that altar that the evangelist joined his faith with mine and would not depart until this experience and empowerment of the Holy Spirit was accomplished. That same man later became my pastor, counselor, and colleague in ministry. And even later became the author of one of the finest works concerning the power of the Holy Spirit I have ever read. That man is Rev. Kenneth McGee…and that book is the one you now hold in your hand.

The only regret I have concerning this written volume is that it was not available when I was a young man seeking God's direction and His plans for my life, both personally and professionally. As a minister, I find myself possessing great concerns about the lack of emphasis on the role of the Holy Spirit in our churches and the lives of those individuals who seek the fullness of God for themselves. As a parent, I pray for my children to know and experience the power of Pentecost in a similar fashion to that which impacted my life as a child and young man. As a leader of today's youth, I hunger for a modern day move of the Spirit of God even greater than the experiences referred to in these chapters.

I can tell you that every testimony and truth communicated in this exciting work will strengthen your faith and motivate you to a greater pursuit of all God has for you as a child of God. I was personally blessed to be present and enjoy many of the great miracles and moves of God described herein. Having been in services with and knowing the author as I do, I am pleased and honored to present the following pages as a gift from God and one of His choice servants…Kenneth McGee.

Tom Greene
National Youth Director
General Council of the Assemblies of God
Springfield, Missouri

INTRODUCTION

Gretnia and I were in revival in Enid, Oklahoma in the early days of our ministry, when I had a dream one night. In my dream, we were driving on a four-lane road, when suddenly, right in front of us a van loaded with people, ran off the road and overturned. We stopped, and I ran to see if I could help. When I asked if there were any thing I could do, the people cried that, "We want someone full of the Holy Spirit to pray for us!" Ever since that night, the Holy Spirit has placed an emphasis in my ministry, on the Holy Spirit. As a result, I have seen thousands filled with the Holy Spirit. I love to preach on the Holy Spirit, and, then pray for people to receive the Baptism. In fact, I have spent more than forty - four years studying and preaching on the subject. Over the years, I have seen more filled with the Holy Spirit in our revivals, than I have seen saved.

There is a tremendous need in our churches today for a Holy Spirit revival. There is not nearly enough preaching on the Holy Spirit. The statistics in our latest ACMR reveals that only 18% of people who were saved this past year were then filled with the Holy Spirit. This is the same percentage of the three previous years. I have watched the trend since 1987, when only 35% of those saved, were filled with the Holy Spirit. This means we are quickly becoming a non-Pentecostal denomination. During the past three years, in our revival meetings, when I asked how many had a current up-to-date experience, with the evidence of speaking in other tongues, not one of our Assembly of God churches had as many as half their congregations who raised their hands.

If we are to change the trend and reach a lost and dyingworld with the gospel, then we must equip ourselves for the task. The Lord has given us the means whereby we can reach them. **"But ye shall receive power, after that the Holy Ghost is come**

upon you: and ye shall be witnesses unto me both in Jerusalem, and in all Judea, and in Samaria, and unto the uttermost part of the earth." Acts 1:8. His desire for us is that we are filled with the Holy Spirit, endued with power from on high, speaking in other tongues as the Spirit gives us utterance.

There are tremendous benefits to those filled with the Holy Spirit. That's what this book is all about.

CHAPTER ONE

What is Pentecost really like?

Do you want to be really Pentecostal? If you do, you sing that way! You don't sing, "Lead kindly light amid the encircling gloom!" You don't sing, "How tedious and tasteless".

You tap your toe and clap your hands on "Amazing Grace How Sweet The Sound!"

You pray in a Pentecostal fashion, unashamed to open your mouth, and praying without worrying about what people around you may think! **I Timothy 2:8 "I will therefore that men pray every where, lifting up holy hands, without wrath and doubting".**

You shout aloud unto the Lord and clap your hands! **Psalms 47:1 "O clap your hands, all ye people; shout unto God with the voice of triumph".**

You praise the Lord in a Pentecostal fashion! **Psalms 107:8 "Oh that men would praise the Lord for his goodness, and for his wonderful works to the children of men!"** The same words are spoken in verses 15, 21, and 31.

Behind every one of those verses is an unusual thing. You have an exclamation point! There are not very many of these in the Bible, but anytime you run across one you had better pause there and listen to what has just been said!

The great heart cry of God is that people would praise the Lord for His goodness!

The Lord is not nervous. He enjoys the praises of His people! **Psalms 22:3 "But thou art holy, O thou that inhabitest the praises of Israel".** The word, **"inhabitest"**, means, **"Art enthroned upon".** The person, who is praising the Lord, lifts by his praises, the Lord above everyone else in the world! He sits on the throne of our heart when we praise Him!

Some people want to be Pentecostal and some don't. I often think about Don and Nita Brankel, my good friends who pastor in Texarkana, Arkansas. You look at their address and wonder: is it Arkansas, or is it Texas? That may be all right for a town, but spiritually, no!

There are people who like to hang in between. They say they are Naza-costal or Bapti-costal or Method-costal or Catho-costal. They try to enjoy the best of both worlds.

The Bible has laid this out so that when you get it, the Baptism of the Holy Spirit, you have something. You may not know at first, exactly what it is, but it is wonderful beyond description.

Acts 2:1 "And when the day of Pentecost was fully come..." I think we should read God's word with an inner feeling of excitement! We're reading the report of the greatest day the world has known since the birth, death and resurrection of our Lord!

The day of Pentecost began at 9 o'clock in the morning. That's the time cloven tongues like as of fire fell upon the 120. We are still living in the day of Pentecost, but now it is approaching the midnight hour. After more than 2000 years, the Holy Spirit is still being mightily outpoured upon the world.

Many today are asking, **"What is Pentecost really like?"**

PENTECOST IS LIKE THE FULFILMENT OF SOMETHING LONGED FOR!

Acts 2:1 "And when the day of Pentecost was fully come, they were all with one accord in one place."

When the 120 gathered in the Upper Room, they had one desire, common among them all: they wanted more from the Lord. They had had wonderful relationships and experiences with the Lord. He had told them there was more available, but for them to receive they must do as He said in **Luke 24:49 "And, behold, I send the promise of my Father upon you: but <u>tarry ye</u> in the city of Jerusalem, until ye be endued with power from on high."** When they gathered in the upper room, they were waiting to receive something from Him. They just didn't know exactly what. They were all in one accord as they waited with great anticipation.

When we are saved, we're given a new heart. **Ezekiel 36:26 "A new heart also will I give you, and a new spirit will I put within you…"** When we receive our new heart, there is a longing instilled in our heart for something more of God. Do you remember how wonderful you felt when you were saved? Do you remember wanting more of the Lord? There is more than just gladness about escaping hell. We want more of God! We begin experiencing what the 120 experienced.

They prayed and tarried and waited until they received. Satisfaction came to them. They were filled with the Holy Spirit.

The Holy Spirit, which draws us to the Lord, begins making us hungry for more and more of Him. When we receive the

Baptism of the Holy Spirit, it is the fulfillment of that longing we have had that cannot be fulfilled in any other way!

Too many in our churches today are satisfied with far less than is available to them! I wonder how many really want more of the Lord? If people want more of the Lord, they have a strange way of showing it. Many churches no longer have Sunday evening services. The people won't come. Evidently, they have too many other things more important to do. What can be more important than drawing closer to Him? What can be more important than being filled with the Holy Spirit?

The Lord has an abundant supply of His power and glory. The key to receiving more is to **"…hunger and thirst after right-eousness"**. That is entirely up to us!

PENTECOST IS LIKE A BIT OF HEAVEN COMING DOWN!

Acts 2:2 "And suddenly there came a <u>sound from heaven </u>as of a rushing mighty wind…" The first evidence the Spirit of the living God was coming among them, in mighty, filling power was this rushing, mighty wind. The word, **"spirit"**, in the Greek is **"pnoe"**, which means, **"breath"**! God was breathing on them! Hallelujah!

The people who believe that God is dead will have to take that lie somewhere else. He is still breathing! **2 Corinthians 3:6 "…for the letter killeth, but the spirit giveth life"**. He breathes life into every service, where He is allowed to do so.

There seems to be a trend in many of our churches where the Holy Spirit is not allowed to be manifested. They do not want any demonstration of the Spirit. They do not want messages in tongues. They do not want interpretations of tongues. People are sent to prayer rooms to seek the Holy Spirit. It's sad when we don't want the moving of the Holy Spirit to interrupt our servic-es. Can you imagine sending the 120 to the **"lower room "** to seek for the Baptism of the Holy Spirit?

Too many pastors are doing away with what made Pentecost what it is today! They don't want to offend the new people who are coming to see what has made us different. We're not different for the sake of being different. We're different because of what we allow the Holy Spirit to do in our midst! The Holy Spirit knows what we need. He moves among us to see that those needs are met.

We experienced a continual move of the Holy Spirit while pasturing Brightmoor Tabernacle in Southfield, Michigan. Our altars were filled, every service, with hungry hearts. People were saved, in every service, for eighteen months. More than four hundred were filled with the Holy Spirit in that same period of time. I have a folder filled with testimonies of those who were miraculously healed. There were times we had to move the altars around because so many were slain under the power of God. We had demon-possessed people delivered from the powers of darkness. Not one time did I consider moving people out of our altar area to go to a prayer room. I wanted our children and young people to witness the moving of the Holy Spirit. Heaven was coming down and I wanted everyone to experience the glory of God!

I'll never forget what the Lord spoke to my heart at the end of an altar service one Sunday evening at Brightmoor. He did not speak in an audible voice, but He spoke to my heart, about the invitation I had just given. As I looked across the congregation, I noticed how many children were in the service. He said, "Give the invitation next Sunday evening for the children." I prayed all that week, preparing my message and heart, for that Sunday evening service. The following Sunday evening, when I gave the invitation, I told the congregation, "this is for children only". I was not prepared for what happened. The entire front of the church was filled with children giving their hearts to the Lord. In fact, the altars were so filled we had to bring them up onto the platform. Many received the Baptism of the Holy

Spirit, with the evidence of speaking in other tongues. It was a glorious service.

One thing that that service produced was the fact that those children did not want to miss our Sunday evening services anymore. As a result, our Sunday evening crowd increased dramatically. No longer could the parents use the excuse they needed to keep their kids home so they could go to bed early.

I believe the thing that drew so many people to our services in Brightmoor was the wonderful move of the Holy Spirit in our altars. He had liberty to move. I wanted Him to direct me as I conducted the services. The Holy Spirit convicted people as they sat in the audience. They responded to the invitation as the Spirit drew them to the altar. God was breathing on us.

That's what Pentecost is really like…being breathed upon by God! Every time there is an outpouring of His Spirit in a service…God is breathing upon us!

Look at the word **"inspiration"**. Can you see the word **"spirit"** there? The word **"inspiration"** means to be **"in-breathed"**!

When you receive the Baptism of the Holy Spirit, you are to be an **"in-breathed"** person…a person inspired by Almighty God! You can tell the difference in a person when they are inspired. There is a fresh anointing resting upon them. God is breathing upon them. There is a fresh surge of power, as their words come alive.

I know there have been times in my own ministry when I thought…wow! Where did that come from? God breathed upon me!

I believe there are many people in our churches to day who need **mouth-to-mouth resuscitation from the Lord!** They are almost gone and they need the Lord to help them breath so there is a sign of life again.

PENTECOST IS LIKE A TOUCH OF PURIFYING FIRE!

Acts 2:3 "And there appeared unto them cloven tongues like as of fire, and it sat upon each of them".

The breath of God had come into the place and filled the whole house where they were **"sitting",** according to verse two. You can get the Baptism anywhere, in any position. I have prayed for people laying on their backs, sitting on an altar or pew, or standing, in response to the invitation.

I remember several years ago when I was preaching a revival in one of our churches in Oklahoma City, a man had come forward several nights, seeking the Baptism. The night he received, I was bending over him, praying, while he was on his back, when suddenly he burst out speaking in tongues. The power of God hit his brother and me at the same time. The people told me after the service what happened at that moment.

They said the two of us began dancing in the Spirit back and forth across the front of the church. People were slain under the power all across the front of the church. They said we never touched anyone as we danced before the Lord. I know that when I realized where I was, I was standing on the platform, facing the baptistery. When the Holy Spirit is in control, everything is done in decency and in order. It had to be the Holy Spirit keeping us from stepping on someone.

Into the upper room came this blazing fire, **"cloven tongues like as of fire".** Like a sheet, it split, into 120 pieces, and sat upon each of them.

Wouldn't it be marvelous if our eyes could behold the burning glory of God that rests upon us when we gather to worship Him, just as it did to those in the Upper Room! **Verse three stated, "And there <u>appeared unto them</u> cloven tongues..."** They actually saw what was happening in the Spirit!

I have often prayed the Lord would let the scales be removed from my eyes, so I could actually see what was happening in our services. In **2 Kings 6:17 "And Elisha prayed, and said, Lord, I pray thee, open his eyes, that he may see. And the Lord opened the eyes of the young man; and he saw: and, behold, the mountain was full of horses and chariots of fire round about Elisha".** When Elisha prayed, the eyes of his servant were opened! I'm convinced there are things happening in all our services that would amaze us, if we could see through the eyes of the Spirit. Lord, open our eyes!

If we could only realize, **God the Father is always in our midst; Revelation 1:8 "I am Alpha and Omega, the beginning and the ending, saith the Lord, which is, and which was, and which is to come, the Almighty". Jesus is always in our midst; Hebrews 13:5 "...for he hath said, I will never leave thee, nor forsake thee". The Holy Spirit is always with us; John 14:16 "And I will pray the Father, and he shall give you another Comforter, that he may abide with you for ever". Angels are with us; Psalms 34:7 "The angel of the Lord encampeth round about them that fear him, and delivered them". Psalms 23:6 "Surely goodness and mercy shall follow me all the days of my life..."**

We have those six with us all the time! That makes seven of us, in every service. Seven is God's perfect number! We have all the ingredients, in every service, for a mighty outpouring of His Holy Spirit.

God intended for us to have the fire of the Almighty burning upon us!

Do you believe it? Do you have it?

God does not need anymore **"unfired"** Pentecostals! He needs people who are on fire, if we are to reach a lost and dying world! Things happen in the fire!

People need to come to church sometime with the expressed purpose of receiving the Baptism of the Holy Spirit.

Several years ago, in a revival at Glad Tiding Assembly of God, Oklahoma City, the pastor's grandson began attending the services. Billy did not have the Baptism of the Holy Spirit, but began seeking each night. As I prayed with him one night, I felt impressed to tell him to come the next night, and pray until he received. When he left, I told him I would also be praying with him.

The next night, when it was time for the service to begin, Billy was not there. A few minutes after the service began, Billy walked in with his girlfriend. When I gave the invitation for those who wanted to receive the Baptism, Billy just stood there. He had not really entered into the service that night as he had been doing.

I felt impressed to go back and talk to him. When I asked him if he had been praying to receive the Baptism that night, he told he had prayed diligently that day. I asked him why he had not come forward at the invitation. He said, "Brother McGee, when my girlfriend and I were on the way to the church, we were so excited about me receiving the Baptism, we could hardly wait to get to church. But, on the way, a car -load of boys pulled up beside us and began saying vulgar things. Brother McGee, I got so mad I could hardly stand it. And, I know, that with my heart feeling that way, it wouldn't do me any good to come forward and try and receive the Baptism."

I told him, "Billy, the devil doesn't want you to receive the Baptism, but now is the time to come." He stepped out, and came to the altar, and it wasn't but just a few minutes until he was speaking in tongues as the Spirit gave him the utterance. The fire was burning, and before the revival was over, more than thirty were saved and more than thirty were filled with the Holy Spirit.
I will not say you have to **see** the fire or **feel** the fire, but you

had better have it!

John the Baptist said in **Matthew 3:11 "I indeed baptize you with water unto repentance: but he that cometh after me is mightier than I, whose shoes I am not worthy to bear: he shall baptize you with the Holy Ghost, and with <u>fire</u>".**
We need to be totally immersed, covered and fully overwhelmed with the living fire of Almighty God, the one who is Himself, the God of fire!

Getting the Baptism is like having a touch of heaven's fire upon your heart!

PENTECOST IS LIKE BEING FULL OF GOD!

Acts 2:4 "And they were all filled with the Holy Ghost, and began to speak with other tongues, as the Spirit gave them utterance."

It is hard to describe something like this; **"Being full of God!"**

God has this, as His will for you, stated by the apostle Paul in **Ephesians 3:19 "...that ye might be filled with all the fullness of God".** What does it mean, **"...Filled with all the fullness of God"?**

When we are born again and accept Jesus Christ as our Saviour, we then have access to Him, who is the Bread of Life! **John 6:35 "And Jesus said unto them, I am the bread of life..."**

Now I want to say this, with all the kindness and reverence of my heart. Bread, as a diet, all by itself; nourishing, satisfying, live-giving as it is, can **become dry!** It is wonderful to have Jesus as our bread of life.

Jesus said, in His temptation, in **Luke 4:4 "...That man shall not live by bread alone..."** It takes more than just bread to be able to live.

You see, there also needs to be water. Jesus spoke about this in **John 7:38,39 "He that believeth on me, as the scripture hath said, out of his belly shall flow rivers of living water. But this spake he of the Spirit, which they that believe on him should receive: for the Holy Ghost was not yet given; because that Jesus was not yet glorified".**

There is nowhere in the entire Bible where it speaks of being **filled with the Father!**

There is not a verse where we are admonished to **be filled with Jesus!** Jesus is wonderful, but it doesn't say to be filled, **"with the Bread" or "Jesus!"**

But, it does say in **Ephesians 5:18 "And be not drunk with wine, wherein is excess; but be <u>filled with the Spirit".</u>**

On the Day of Pentecost, in **Acts 2:4 "And they were all filled with the Holy Ghost, and began to speak with other tongues, as the Spirit gave them utterance".**

The Holy Spirit is the filling portion of the Godhead!

We cannot have all the fullness of God in our lives, until we have received the filling portion of the Godhead, the Blessed Third Person of the Triune Godhead!

We are not to live substandard to the plan and will of God in our lives!

PENTECOST IS LIKE HAVING TWO PEOPLE SPEAKING AT ONCE!

Acts 2:4 "And they were all filled with the Holy Ghost, and began to speak with other tongues, as the Spirit gave them utterance".

On the Day of Pentecost, 120 received the Baptism of the Holy Spirit, speaking in other tongues as the Spirit gave them utterance. **The Holy Spirit did not speak one word!** You cannot quote one word the Holy Spirit said in the entire account.

Do you know what they were doing? They were magnifying God and giving Him glory. They were lost in their God. Heaven was coming down. They were getting blessed, and the people who heard them speaking all different languages, were getting blessed!

The Holy Spirit gave them the words to say, and they gave it the sound! That's the only way He has of speaking. He uses our voice, our lips, our tongue, and our mind. He quickens our mind, so the words can be spoken. **But, we do the speaking!**

Anytime someone tries to tell you what to say in other tongues, just so you can get in the habit of speaking in other tongues, they have flubbed it from the start! People may mean well, but they are wrong, in trying to do so.

You must yield yourself to the speaking member of the Godhead, and, He gives you words to say to the lover of your soul, Jesus Christ, Himself. If He can't furnish you the words, you will never get them.

If someone else furnishes the words for you, they are flesh. It is not the Holy Spirit! The Holy Spirit gives us exactly what He wants us to say!

When you are talking to the Lord, and the Holy Spirit begins giving you that heavenly language, cloven tongues like as of fire, you are saying things to God that only by the Spirit could be said.

It has to please the Lord. It has to bless Him. It has to be just what He wants to hear, because the Holy Spirit knows all things and is able to give us what the Lord wants to hear!

It's like two people speaking at once!

You don't take a correspondence course on how to speak in tongues. **He** gives you the words, and **you,** give them the utterance. It is supernatural, and yet, in a sense, it is natural. It is the holy merging of the person who is being filled, and the Holy Spirit, who comes in, in fullness. When you get through, He has given you the words!

There is also a maturing process. You may have an initial experience, where you only speak one or two words, over and over. Let me urge you, don't doubt it! As you continue to yield, the Holy Spirit will give you more and more words.

Our children start speaking slowly. They add a word here and there, but eventually, they're speaking clearly and distinctly. They are learning, they are maturing. We will do the same thing as we continue to yield to the Spirit.

For those who have received the Holy Spirit, you may have found that since you initially received, that through the years your language has changed. We don't change it just anytime we want to, it has to be the Holy Spirit doing the changing.

I'll never forget one night, several years ago, in a revival in Lewis Avenue Assembly of God in Tulsa, Oklahoma. The Lord was moving in a special way. I felt He was trying to do something in our midst, but the people were quenching the Spirit.

We had been told, in the beginning of the service, that we had special guests there that night. The pastor had introduced the pastor of one of the large evangelical churches in the area. We all knew that they did not believe in speaking in tongues. As a result, the people were not entering into worship the way they had been doing.

When the pastor turned the service to me, I asked the piano player to give me an E-flat chord. I told the people, if they were ashamed of the Lord, to just stand still. But, if they were not ashamed of Him, I wanted them to start marching around the church, as we sang, "When The Saints Go Marching In".

I'll never forget the response, as the congregation began singing and marching around the sanctuary. There was a tremendous outpouring of the Holy Spirit. People began shouting and praising the Lord. The piano player suddenly fell off the piano bench, slain under the power of God. When he hit the floor, he was speaking in tongues. The Lord had baptized him with the Holy Spirit. He received an experience he had never had before.

I looked over at the delegation from the evangelical church. The pastor had brought several of his elders with him. One of the elders had brought his sister with him. They all had come because some people in their congregation had friends and relatives who were members of Lewis Avenue, and had been told what the Lord was doing in the revival services. They had come that night to check us out!

The sister of one of the elders stepped out and got in the Jericho march, as the people marched around the church. As she approached the front of the church, she stopped directly in front of me, and with tears coursing down her checks, asked, " **Would the Lord give me what these people have?"**

I told her that He would, if she would only ask and begin praising Him. She immediately began praising the Lord, asking Him to fill her with the Holy Spirit. It wasn't but just a few minutes, and she burst out speaking in tongues.

When she received the Baptism, the pastor and elders, including her brother, came and watched as the Holy Spirit moved mightily upon her. She went from one language to another, as the Holy Spirit flowed. There was no doubt that it was the Holy Spirit! She simply spoke as the Spirit gave her the words.

I wish I could tell you the pastor from the evangelical church received the Baptism that night, but he did not. However, within a few weeks, he too, received the Holy Spirit, with the evidence of speaking in other tongues.

When you receive the Baptism, and begin speaking in other tongues, you are saying what the Holy Spirit gives you to say! It is like two people speaking at once!

PENTECOST IS LIKE BEING FULL OF WINE!

Acts 2:13-16 "Others mocking said, These men are full of new wine. But Peter, standing up with the eleven, lifted up his voice, and said unto them, Ye men of Judea, and all ye that dwell at Jerusalem, be this known unto you, and hearken to my words: For these are not drunken, as ye suppose, seeing it is but the third hour of the day. But this is that which was spoken by the prophet Joel:"

In the Bible, wine is the essence of joy! There was great joy on the Day of Pentecost!

In all the years I have prayed for people to receive the Baptism, I have never seen anyone unhappy at the moment they received the Holy Spirit! In fact, exactly the opposite has been true. I have seen them laughing, crying, shouting, running, staggering and falling prostrate. But, I have never seen them unhappy.

The people, who observed the 120 on the Day of Pentecost, came to the conclusion, that they were drunk!

I'm not putting any premium on acting weird. According to the world's standards, you and I are about a half a bubble off level anyway. They look at us and say; "I've never seen anything like that in my life!

Can you imagine what people from cold, dead, old-line, lethargic churches think when they come to visit our services? They come, and we are praising the Lord, lifting our hands, clapping, hugging each other, telling each other we love them, and laughing in the Spirit, speaking in tongues. They have never seen anything like it.

It's like something this world doesn't know about - to be filled with the Spirit! There is joy, like the sweet wine of heaven, being poured into our hearts.

When people in the world get drunk, they can become deadly. Drunk drivers, every year, kill thousands. Thousands others are maimed.

The world says, "Oh, they are just having a good time", as they laugh at people who are drunk.

The scenes you see on T.V. are always young people, supposedly having a wonderful time, drinking "Bud-dumber". You are never shown the scene of the next morning, getting out of bed with a hangover, having a splitting headache, amid their own vomit. The world tries to tell us that, that is the normal thing.

When we get filled with the Holy Spirit, we become soul-winners. We don't destroy people's lives, we try to save them.

Peter didn't say they weren't drunk. He said they weren't drunk as they thought. He said they were full of the Holy Spirit and that is like being full of new wine!

PENTECOST IS LIKE THE FULFILLING OF PROPHECY IN YOUR LIFE!

Acts 2:17,18 "And it shall come to pass in the last days, saith God, I will pour out of my Spirit upon all flesh: and your sons and your daughters shall prophesy, and your young men shall have visions, and your old men shall dream dreams: And on my servants and on my handmaidens I will pour out in those days of my Spirit; and they shall prophesy:"

I can tell you, this is the fulfilling of prophecy!

The great prophet, Joel, 750 B.C., is speaking of the great out-pouring of the Holy Spirit. For these are his words, recorded here in the book of Acts. He said, **"In the last days, (There is no doubt we are in the last days), saith God, (Look who is speaking), I will pour out of my Spirit upon <u>all flesh,</u> (Not just some, but all): and your sons and your daughters shall prophesy, (I long to see that among our young people).** It seems that many of our young people are not being given the privilege of seeing an outpouring of the Holy Spirit in their services.

I have a missionary friend of mine who has returned to the United States, who called me and told me it was alarming to him, that in many of the churches he was visiting, many of the young people had not been in an old-fashion Holy Spirit serv-ice. He told me many of the youth had not even heard messages on the Baptism of the Holy Spirit.

We cannot expect our young men and women to prophesy and speak in tongues if they are never exposed to the message. All too often, we let them experience it in youth camps, but not in our church services.

There is no doubt in this passage, that God wants an outpouring upon all ages. This is a marvelous picture of a tremendous gushing and outpouring from another world.

Joel said it would come to pass, and, on the Day of Pentecost, it came to pass. Ever since that day, there have been Pentecostal believers who have staggered out of upper rooms, under the impact of Almighty God! There are more Pentecostal believers in the world today than there have ever been!

The largest churches in the world today are tongue talking, Spirit-filled churches! It's exciting to see what the Lord is doing!

God didn't say, "In the last days, I will sprinkle a bit of the Spirit, here and there, about in the world". He said, **"I will pour out of my Spirit upon all flesh"!** He is not a respecter of persons concerning the outpouring of the Holy Spirit. He wants everyone to have the Baptism.

When you have received the Baptism of the Holy Spirit, you have received for yourself, the fulfillment of prophecy of the great prophet Joel!

PENTECOST IS LIKE HAVING GOD, IN ALL HIS GLORY, POURING OVER YOU!

Acts 2:18 "And on my servants and on my handmaidens I will pour out in those days of my Spirit; and they shall prophesy:"

There is a reason why we receive the Baptism! **Well, for one thing, it feels so good!**

There is no such thing as **"holy numbness".** There are a lot of people today, who are numb, who used to have the Holy Spirit. You need to keep your experience up-to-date.

Here is the reason why you need to keep your experience current! **Acts 1:8 "But ye shall receive power, after that the Holy Ghost is come upon you: and ye shall be witnesses unto me both in Jerusalem, and in all Judea, and in Samaria, and unto the uttermost part of the earth".**
There is a job to do, that you cannot do, without the Holy Spirit! God has a plan for you, in your home, work, neighborhood, which cannot be accomplished apart from the Holy Spirit!

There is no substitute for the power of the Holy Spirit! The arm of flesh will fail. God never intended for us to win battles in the arm of the flesh.

When we receive the **"power"** of the Holy Spirit, we receive "miracle force, miraculous ability, great abundance, mighty strength and miraculous violence against the enemy"! All these meanings are included in the word, "power" in the Greek.

This is all available because God is pouring Himself out upon us!

STUDY QUESTIONS FOR CHAPTER ONE

What does it mean to praise the Lord in "Pentecostal fashion"? Cite appropriate scriptures and explain.

Name three spiritual attributes or practices that are present in a believer's life that demonstrate a longing for the Pentecostal experience.

What is meant by the statement "the Holy Spirit breathed upon the congregation."

Explain the word in-breathed as it relates to the word inspiration.

What is meant by the statement "Pentecost is like a touch of purifying fire"?

Explain the portion of scripture that states "and there appeared unto them cloven tongues like as of fire" (Acts 2:3).

Explain the statement "Pentecost is like being 'Full of God.'"

When one is filled with the Spirit who does the speaking? Who is the filling portion of the Godhead? Explain what is meant by the statement "it is like two people speaking at once."

Explain the statement "Pentecost is like the fulfilling of prophecy in your life." What was the prophet goal's role in foretelling the Great Day of Pentecost.

List five reasons why we should receive the Holy Spirit?

CHAPTER TWO

What is the Baptism with the Holy Spirit

I am amazed at the confusion of many people concerning the baptism with the Holy Spirit. However, I know I have been blessed to have been raised in Pentecost, where many have not had that privilege. As a result, I want to try and answer some questions people may have about the subject.

The first question I will try to answer is "what is The Baptism with the Holy Spirit" or "what is the Baptism with the Holy Ghost"? By the way, these two terms are used synonymously. In **Acts 1:2 "Until the day in which he was taken up, after that he through the Holy Ghost had given commandment unto the apostles whom he had chosen".** The term **"Holy Ghost"**, as used in this setting, shows that the Holy Spirit is now the agent and executive of God in earth to carry on the work that the Father gave Him to do. The two words **"Ghost"** and **"Spirit"** are the same in the Greek. The Greek word is "pneuma". You will find this term, **"Holy Ghost",** throughout the King James translation, while in the NIV and other translations, it is translated **"Holy Spirit"**. Throughout our study I will use the two terms interchangeably.

The Baptism with the Holy Spirit is a definite experience which we will know whether or not we have received. This is clear from **Acts 1:4,5 "And, being assembled together with them, commanded them that they should not depart from**

Jerusalem, but wait for the promise of the Father, which, saith he, ye have heard of me. For John truly baptized with water; but ye shall be baptized with the Holy Ghost not many days hence".

If it were not possible to know if you were filled or not, how could the disciples have known when the days of waiting were over, and, the days to begin their ministry had begun?

The same thing is clear from **Acts 19:2 "He said unto them, Have ye received the Holy Ghost since ye believed? And they said unto him, We have not so much as heard whether there be any Holy Ghost".**

Paul had gone to the city of Ephesus and found a small group of disciples, twelve in number, **Acts 19:7.** There was something about these twelve disciples that did not satisfy Paul. We are not told exactly what it was. It may have been there was not that abounding joy about them that one expects to find in Spirit-filled Christians. It may have been that Paul was troubled by the fact that there were only twelve of them, thinking that if they were Spirit-filled, there would certainly have been more than twelve of them at this time.

Whatever it was that disturbed Paul, he went right to the root of the difficulty by putting to them, the question that we have just read, **"have ye received the Holy Ghost since ye believed"?** I believe Paul expected a definite "Yes" or a definite "No" to that question.

There is a lot of talk today about the Baptism of the Holy Spirit and much prayer about the Holy Spirit that is vague and indefinite.

I have been in revival services where I prayed for people to receive the Baptism of the Holy Spirit, and afterwards I asked them if they received the Baptism, and they would say, "Well, I hope so".

The Bible is definite about salvation! It is so definite that if a man is saved and knows his Bible, he can say, "yes, the Lord in His infinite mercy has saved me".

Paul was sure of his experience. He said in **2 Timothy 1:12 "...for I know whom I have believed, and am persuaded that he is able to keep that which I have committed unto him against that day".** There was no doubt in his mind about his experience and relationship with the Lord.

The Bible is just as definite about the Baptism with the Holy Spirit! It is so definite that if a man has been "baptized with the Holy Spirit", and knows his Bible, he can answer, "Yes, the Lord in His infinite mercy has filled me with the Holy Spirit".

Peter stood on the Day of Pentecost, after having received the Baptism with the Holy Spirit, and gave the first apostolic sermon, declaring in **Acts 2:16, "But this is that which was spoken by the prophet Joel".** He gave a direct reference to the Baptism with the Holy Spirit, which Joel had given in 795-755 B.C. He knew what he had received! He stated in **Acts 2:39 "For the promise is unto you, and to your children, and to all that are afar off, even as many as the Lord our God shall call".** He was saying, "it's not just for me, it's for everyone."

It is possible that a man may be saved, and, by reason of his ignorance of the Bible, not have the assurance of his salvation. I have dealt with many people over the years, which questioned their salvation experience, because they didn't "feel it". They were looking for something someone else may have experienced. They couldn't accept their salvation because they didn't know the Scriptures. Salvation is not a feeling; it is not an emotion. Salvation is a gift. **Ephesians 2:8 "For by grace are ye saved through faith; and that not of yourselves: it is the gift of God".** Salvation comes by faith. Salvation comes by believing.

It is quite possible that a man may have been "baptized with the

Holy Spirit" and yet, through ignorance of the Bible, not know the name of the experience he has received. Again, I have dealt with many people over the years, who, when I asked what happened to them, after hearing them speak in tongues, would say, "Well, I don't know for sure what has happened". Sadly, many would never accept what the Lord had done for them, all because they didn't know the Scriptures. The Scriptures state in **Acts 2:3,4 "And there appeared unto them cloven tongues like as of fire, and it sat upon each of them. And they were all filled with the Holy Ghost, and began to speak with other tongues, as the Spirit gave them utterance".** The Baptism with the Holy Spirit comes by faith. It comes by believing.

The Baptism with the Holy Spirit is a work of the Holy Spirit, distinct from, and additional to, His regenerating work. It is one thing to be born again by the Holy Spirit, and quite another thing to be baptized with the Holy Spirit!

It is evident from **Acts 1:5 "For John truly baptized with water; but ye shall be baptized with the Holy Ghost not many days hence",** that the apostles had not yet been baptized with the Holy Spirit. But, they were to be "not many days hence".

The men to whom our Lord spoke were already regenerate men. When given the opportunity to follow Him, without exception, began following Him. He called Peter and Andrew in **Matthew 4:18-20.** He said, **"Follow me, and I will make you fishers of men".** They left their nets, and followed Jesus. Leaving all is required of all men if we become His disciples.

He called James and John in **Matthew 4:21,22.** Verse 22 stated **"And they immediately left the ship and their father, and followed him".** Jesus said in **Matthew 10:37 "He that loveth father or mother more than me is not worthy of me: and he that loveth son or daughter more than me is not worthy of me".** Jesus was talking about total commitment to Him. James and John left the means of their livelihood and their family to follow Jesus.

So, it was evident that the apostles were regenerate men. They had left all to follow Him. Unregenerate men do not leave all to follow Jesus. These men were already born again, but they were not baptized with the Holy Spirit.

Every believer has the Holy Spirit for He dwells in every one that is born again. This appears clearly in **Romans 8:9 "But ye are not in the flesh, but in the Spirit, if so be that the Spirit of God dwell in you. Now if any man have not the Spirit of Christ, he is none of his"**.

You can be baptized with the Holy Spirit at the same time you are born again. This happened in the household of Cornelius in **Acts 10.** Cornelius and his household and friends were listening to the first gospel sermon they had ever heard in their lives. Peter had come to the climax of his sermon in **Acts 10:43,** where he says: **"To him [to the Lord Jesus] give all the prophets witness, that through his name whosoever believeth in him shall receive remission of sins"**.

No sooner had Peter spoken those words than they all believed on the Lord Jesus and were born again. And then, before Peter could finish his sermon, we read **verses 44-46, "While Peter yet spake these words, the Holy Ghost fell on all them which heard the word. And they of the circumcision which believed were astonished, as many as came with Peter, because that on the Gentiles also was poured out the gift of the Holy Ghost. For they heard them speak with tongues, and magnify God..."** So, we see that they were baptized with the Holy Spirit the very moment they believed, and were born again.

I believe this should be the normal experience in the Church today, but the Church is not in a normal order today! This is evident by the fact that only eighteen percent of people being saved in our churches today, are then filled with the Holy Spirit, according to the Annual Church Ministries Report of the Assemblies of God for 2002.

The Baptism with the Holy Spirit is a work of the Holy Spirit always connected with, and, primarily for the purpose of testimony and service.

This is evident from the passage where the Lord Jesus made the original promise of the Baptism with the Holy Spirit in **Acts 1:8 "But ye shall receive power, after that the Holy Ghost is come upon you: and ye shall be witnesses unto me both in Jerusalem, and in all Judea, and in Samaria, and unto the uttermost part of the earth".**

There is not one single passage in the Bible, either in the Old Testament or the New Testament, where the Baptism with the Holy Spirit is spoken of, where it is not connected with testimony or service.

The Baptism with the Holy Spirit is not primarily for the purpose of making us individually holy. I am not saying that it is not the work of the Holy Spirit to make us holy, for it is His work to make us holy, and it is only through His work that any of us can become holy. **But, the primary purpose of the Baptism with the Holy Spirit is to equip us and fit us for service!**

It is not the primary purpose of the Baptism with the Holy Spirit to make us personally happy. I am not saying that the Baptism with the Holy Spirit will not make us happy. I have never known anyone yet, who was baptized with the Holy Spirit, into whose heart a new and more wonderful joy did not come. **The primary purpose of the Baptism with the Holy Spirit is to make us useful for God!**

I would rather go my entire life without one single touch of ecstasy or rapture, and have power to do my part to stem this awful tide and save at least some, than to have indescribable raptures every day of my life, and have no power to win the lost.

I want to be very clear and emphatic at this point, for here is where many people today are going astray. Men and women go to Bible conferences, to meetings for the deepening of spiritual life, to extended revival meetings, and to tarrying meetings, and they come back and tell you what a wonderful experience they have had, and how they have been baptized with the Holy Spirit. But, many of these people are of no more use to their pastors or their churches than they were before they left. They have no more love for souls than they had before. They make no more effort for the salvation of the lost than they did before. They win no more souls to the Lord than they did before.

I am not quite sure what kind of experience they may have had in these meetings, but they have not had the Baptism with the Holy Spirit along the lines so plainly laid out in God's Word!

The results of the Baptism with the Holy Spirit, as set forth in the Word of God are many-fold, but they can all be summed up in one word, and that word is "**POWER**"!

This is revealed in the passage to which I have already referred, **Acts 1:8 "But ye shall receive power after that the Holy Ghost is come upon you..."**. This power will not manifest itself in the same way in every individual.

There are some that feel that all they need to become an evangelist is to receive the Baptism with the Holy Spirit. That is simply the error of presumption. It takes more than being baptized with the Holy Spirit to become an evangelist. In order to be an evangelist, the first thing a person needs is a call from God to that specific work. While it is true that everyone who is saved **should** become a soul-winner and those who are baptized with the Holy Spirit **should** receive power to be witnesses, it still requires a call from the Lord to become an evangelist.

The second thing a person needs in order to be an evangelist, is such knowledge of the Word of God, that they have something to preach, to which it is worth listening.

One of the most unfortunate things in evangelistic work today is so many have rushed into the work whom God never called. They may have received the baptism with the Holy Spirit, and mistaken the call to win souls, to thinking they were called to be an evangelist.

I had a lady in one of the churches, where I was pastor at the time, which had come from another denomination. She received the Baptism with the Holy Spirit and thought the Lord had called her into the ministry. She was so excited with her new experience, but mistaken her newfound enthusiasm for souls, to believing the Lord had called her to a special ministry. She had the money to purchase time on a radio station and began a call-in prayer ministry. It lasted for a little while, but then it was discontinued. Our call must come from the Lord and not from our own personal desires to do something for Him.

In our revival meetings, I have had people come to me after being greatly blessed, or after receiving the Baptism with the Holy Spirit, and tell me they felt the Lord had called them into the ministry.

I remember one lady who had several children, who came to me after being blessed in a service, and told me the Lord had called her to be an evangelist, and that she wanted to travel and preach the gospel.

I tried to explain to her that the Lord had already given her a tremendous calling. I told her she had a wonderful family and she had a responsibility to raise her children to know and serve the Lord. I said if she would do that, she could stand one day in the presence of the Lord and hear Him say, "Well done, thou good and faithful servant".

If a mother gets the right conception of the Baptism with the Holy Spirit, then she can say, "evangelist may need the Baptism with the Holy Spirit, my pastor may need the Baptism with the Holy Spirit, but I must have it in order that I may have the power to bring my children up in the nurture and admonition of the Lord".

I think one of the saddest things in the church today is to see the sons and daughters of Christian fathers and mothers, some who have been pillars in the church, growing up not following in the footsteps of their parents. They grow up sometimes quite godless, not in church on the Lord's day, not in Sunday school. Instead of being in church, they are out hunting or fishing, or at the beach or lake, or playing golf or tennis, or joy riding, or the Lord only knows what.

What all mothers, or us fathers need, first of all, is power to get into the hearts of our own children. We can have that power. **Acts 1:8** tells us how: **"But ye shall receive power, after that the Holy Ghost is come upon you..."**.

I have always felt that, as a minister of the gospel, if I were to win the whole world, yet loose my own children, I would be a failure. I need the power of the Holy Spirit to help me be the father I need to be, to be the preacher I need to be, to be the pastor or evangelist I need to be, to be the husband I need to be. The Lord has made it possible for all of us to be what He wants us to be. **Be filled with the Baptism of the Holy Spirit!**

STUDY QUESTIONS FOR CHAPTER TWO

What does the term, "Holy Ghost", mean in its setting in Acts 1:2?

Can you know you have been baptized with the Holy Spirit? If so, how do you know?

How can one be sure about his experience of salvation?

It is stated the Baptism with the Holy Spirit comes about by what two ways?

What is the difference between salvation and the Baptism with the Holy Spirit?

What Scripture reveals the fact that the Holy Spirit dwells in one who is born again?

Where is the evidence found that it is possible to be baptized with the Holy Spirit at the same time you are saved?

What are some of the purposes of being baptized with the Holy Spirit?

What should be the greatest change in your life, once you have been baptized with the Holy Spirit?

What are two things that are important, if you are called to be an evangelist? Is one more important than the other?

What is the great need of mothers and fathers if they are to reach their children, and how do they get it?

CHAPTER THREE

*Who needs the Baptism
with the Holy Spirit
and who can have it?*

The Bible answers this question very plainly. I want us to go to **Luke 24:45-49** and begin with verse 45 to get the connection. **"And opened he their understanding, that they might understand the scriptures. And said unto them, Thus it is written, and thus it behoved Christ to suffer, and to rise from the dead the third day: And that repentance and remission of sins should be preached in his name among all nations, beginning at Jerusalem. And ye are witnesses of these things. And behold, I send the promise of my Father upon you; but tarry ye in the city of Jerusalem, until ye be endued with power from on high"**.

Jesus gave a definite, distinct and positive commandment to the disciples. He said that they should not undertake the work to which He had called them, until they had received the all-necessary preparation for that work, of which He speaks as "the promise of my Father upon you". He said to wait until they were "endued with power from on high".

By comparing Scripture with Scripture we find that this "promise of the Father", this being "endued with power from on high", is the Baptism with the Holy Spirit.

Now, to whom were these words spoken? They were spoken to

the eleven disciples. Who were those disciples? There are some that would say they were uneducated men. Nothing could be further from the truth. They had taken more than a three-year course in the best theological seminary that ever existed upon the earth, and in which our Lord Jesus was the sole, but all-sufficient Teacher. They had been eyewitnesses of our Lord's wondrous life on earth. They were eyewitnesses of His miracles. They were eyewitnesses of His death. They were eyewitnesses of His resurrection from the dead. And, they were about to be eyewitnesses of His ascension.

What were His disciples to do? They were to simply go and tell a perishing world what their own eyes had seen and what their own ears had heard from the lips of the Master Himself. Were they not already fully prepared to go? With our modern ideas of preparation for the ministry we should say they were the most fully and perfectly prepared and equipped men who ever undertook the ministry of the Gospel.

But, our Lord says here: you are not adequately prepared at all. There is another preparation so very important, that you must not take one more step, until you have obtained it. That preparation is the receiving of the "promise of the Father", the being "endued with power from on high", the Baptism with the Holy Spirit. And, He said, "Until you receive it, do not undertake that ministry".

The word translated "tarry" means literally "sit down". "Sit down, until you are endued (clothed) with power from on high".

If our Lord would not permit the men whom He had chosen Himself and ordained for this work to undertake that work until they had received a definite enduement of power from on high for that service, what is it for ordinary people like you or me to undertake that service, until we too, are baptized by the Holy Spirit?

I think one of the big mistakes the church makes today is the way we set men apart for the ministry of the Gospel. We take someone who may feel an interest in the ministry and send them to four years to a Bible College or university and expect them to be ready to cope with all the things they will face in the ministry. They graduate, and we say, "you are now ready", and we lay our hands upon them and set them apart for this solemn work.

But, are they prepared? They are not prepared, if four years of training is all they have. Before we ordain them, we should ask them the questions "are you sure you have been endued with power from on high, Are you sure you have been baptized with the Holy Spirit"? And, if they are not sure, we should say to them, as Jesus said to His disciples, "sit down until you are endued with power from on high".

Look at **Acts 10:38 "How God anointed Jesus of Nazareth with the Holy Ghost and with power: who went about doing good, and healing all that were oppressed of the devil; for God was with him".** To what definite experience does this refer in the life of our Lord as recorded in the Gospels?

Now, turn to **Luke 3:21-22 "Now when all the people were baptized, it came to pass, that Jesus also being baptized, and praying, the heaven was opened, And the Holy Ghost descended in a bodily shape like a dove upon him, and a voice came from heaven, which said, Thou art my beloved Son; in thee I am well pleased".**

And, let's turn to **Luke 4:1 "And Jesus being full of the Holy Ghost returned from Jordan, and was led by the Spirit into the wilderness".**

Now turn to **Luke 4:14-20 "And Jesus returned in the power of the Spirit into Galilee: and there went out a fame of him through all the region round about. And he taught in their synagogues, being glorified of all. And he came to Nazareth, where he had been brought up: and, as his custom was, he** went into the synagogue on the Sabbath day, and stood up for to read. And there was delivered unto him the book of the prophet Esaias. And when he had opened the book, he found the place where it was written, The Spirit of the Lord is upon me, because he hath anointed me to preach the gospel to the poor; he hath sent me to heal the brokenhearted, to preach deliverance to the captives, and recovering of sight to the blind, to set at liberty them that are bruised, To preach the acceptable year of the Lord. And he closed the book, and he gave it again to the minister, and sat down. And the eyes of all them that were in the synagogue were fastened on him".

From these verses we learn that it was at the Jordan that the Lord was endued with power from on high. There is where He received the Holy Spirit. And, after that, and not until that time, did He begin His public ministry.

Who was our Lord? He was the only begotten Son of God. He was God manifested in the flesh. He had been supernaturally conceived by the power of the Holy Spirit. But, He was at the same time man, and as a man, setting an example to you and me to follow in His steps. He never undertook the public ministry, for which He came into this world, until He had been definitely "endued with power from on high".

If Jesus did not permit Himself to undertake His public ministry until He was definitely "endued with power from on high", what is it for ordinary people, such as you and I, to undertake service for Him until we also are endued with power, and know it?

In view of what the Lord required of His Disciples, and still more in view of what He required of Himself, we dare not undertake service for Him until we too, have been filled with the Holy Spirit, and know it!

But, even that is not all! In **Acts 8,** Philip had gone to the city of Samaria and verse 5 states," **preached Christ unto them**".

When the disciples came to a new church that had just begun meeting, the first thing they wanted to do was to get the members of that new church filled with the Holy Spirit. That is evident in **Acts 8:12-17 "But when they believed Philip preaching the things concerning the kingdom of God, and the name of Jesus Christ, they were baptized, both men and women. Then Simon himself believed also: and when he was baptized, he continued with Philip, and wondered, beholding the miracles and signs, which were done. Now when the apostles which were at Jerusalem heard that Samaria had received the word of God, they sent unto them Peter and John: Who, when they were come down, prayed for them, that they might receive the Holy Ghost: (For as yet he was fallen upon none of them: only they were baptized in the name of the Lord Jesus.) Then laid they their hands on them, and they received the Holy Ghost.** It was evident they had been saved and baptized in water, but had not been baptized with the Holy Spirit. Peter and John knew that if they were to build a church, they would need the Baptism with the Holy Spirit.

We may have been baptized with the Holy Spirit, but we need to be refilled many times to help us with each new emergency we face in Christian service.

We are told Peter, in **Acts 2:4,** was among those filled with the Holy Spirit on the Day of Pentecost.

But, In **Acts 4:31 "And when they had prayed, the place was shaken where they were assembled together; and they were all filled with the Holy Ghost, and they spake the word of God with boldness".** Peter and John were in the group that had assembled together to pray, and they were all refilled with the Holy Spirit! The tense of the verb, "filled", used in the Greek, shows conclusively that the filling spoken of here was a new filling that took place right then and there

In fact, in **Acts 4:8 "Then Peter, filled with the Holy Ghost, said unto them…"** again you have the tense of the verb used, to show it was a refilling, that took place then and there.

So here are three separate occasions on which Peter was "filled with the Holy Spirit". It is clear from these passages of Scripture that one needs repeated fillings with the Holy Spirit, no matter how wonderfully he may have been baptized with the Holy Spirit in the past!

We need to be filled again and again, filled anew for each new emergency of Christian service. One of the greatest mistakes we make today, is that many people are trying to work today in the power of some baptism with the Holy Spirit that they received years ago.

I urge you, don't make that same mistake today. No matter how wonderful your experience may have been in the past, you need, you must have, a new infilling for each new challenge you face.

And, we must seek it in God's appointed way. We seek the infilling by prayer, definite prayer for a definite blessing. **Luke 11:13 "If ye then, being evil, know how to give good gifts unto your children: how much more shall your heavenly Father give the Holy Spirit to them that ask him"?**

It is a terrible thing to lose one's anointing. But, we will lose our anointing unless we seek a new filling of the Spirit for each challenge we face.

Now I want to answer the question, **"Who can have the Baptism with the Holy Spirit"?**

The Lord Himself answers the question in the plainest words. Look at **Acts 2:39,** and you will get the Lord's answer to this all-important question. **"For the promise is unto you, and to your children, and to all that are afar off, even as many as the Lord our God shall call".**

What is the "promise" to which Peter refers in this verse? There are two differing interpretations of this verse.

One interpretation is that "the promise " of this verse is the promise of salvation and that the verse therefore sets forth the Covenant privilege of believers to have their children saved.

The other interpretation is that "the promise" of this verse is the promise of the baptism with the Holy Spirit.

Which of these two interpretations is correct?

I was taught in Bible school that there are two laws of interpretation universally accepted by all rational and intelligent interpreters of the Word.

The first law is called **"the law of usage"**. The "law of usage" is that when you find a word or phrase in the Bible and you want to know exactly what it means, the thing to do is not to run for a dictionary to get the definition of the word or phrase, because Bible scholars did not write the dictionary. The thing to do is take your concordance and look up every place in the Bible where that word or phrase is used and interpret its meaning by its usage.

Now what is the usage of this phrase "the promise", in the Bible, especially what is the usage in this particular book in the Bible, in which this verse is found?

Let's look at **Acts 1:4-5 "He charged them not to depart from Jerusalem, but to wait for the promise of the Father, which said He, ye heard from me: for John indeed baptized with water: but ye shall be baptized with the Holy Ghost not many days hence".**

We do not have to guess about what is referred to here in this portion of Scripture as "the promise". We are told that "the promise" is "the promise" of being "baptized with the Holy Spirit".

Let's go next to **Acts 2:33 "Being therefore by the right hand of God exalted and having received of the Father the promise of the Holy Ghost, He hath poured forth this which ye see and hear"**.

Here again we are told that "the promise of the Father" is the "promise of the Holy Ghost" which had just been poured forth on that very day when every one of the apostolic company had been baptized with the Holy Spirit. The meaning of the expression is exactly the same here as it was in the first chapter. Now, just six verses further down, we come to the verse we are now studying.

Can anyone tell me any reasonable rule of interpretation by which this peculiar expression can mean one thing in **Acts1: 4-5**, exactly the same thing in the next place where it occurs, that is**, Acts 2:33**, and something entirely different in the next place where it occurs, only six verses further down?

Now I want us to apply **"the law of context".** The law of context is this: when you find a passage of Scripture where there are two or more possible interpretations, and you want to know which one of the several different interpretations is the correct interpretation, you should look at the passage in its context. That is, look at it in the light of what goes before it and in the light of what comes after it.

There are many passages in the Bible, where if it stood alone, might mean two, three, four or even more things. But, standing where it does, can mean only one thing.

Let us read what goes immediately before, in **verse 38 "Then Peter said unto them, Repent, and be baptized every one of you in the name of Jesus Christ for the remission of sins, and ye shall receive the gift of the Holy Ghost".**

Here, Peter in the preceding verse, declares exactly what the promise is, to which he refers in **verse 39.** He says: "**Ye shall** receive the gift of the Holy Ghost", "For the promise is unto you, and to your children, and to all that are afar off, even as many as the Lord our God shall call".

The promise then, is unmistakably, the promise of the "gift of" or to use the synonymous phrase, "the baptism with" the Holy Spirit.

The two laws therefore agree, and they both determine beyond the possibility of any question, that the promise of **Acts 2:39,** is the promise of the baptism with the Holy Spirit.

Let us now read the verse in the light of this settled fact. "**For unto you is the promise…**" that is, to the people whom he was addressing, who were for the most part Jews. So far there is nothing in it for you and me, for we were not there, and we are not Jews.

But, Peter did not stop there: "**…and to your children**", that is, to the next generation of Jews, or, if you will, to all coming generations of Jews. That doesn't take in many of us yet.

But, Praise the Lord, Peter did not stop there, but added: "**…and to all that are afar off**". That takes us in, for we are the Gentiles "**…who sometimes were far off are made nigh by the blood of Christ**", Ephesians 2:13.

Peter did not leave any doubts about who else was included, but added: "**…even as many as the Lord our God shall call**". We are told here in clear, easy to understand words, the meaning that is unmistakable, the Baptism with the Holy Spirit is for every child of God, in every age of the Church's history!

The Baptism with the Holy Spirit is the birthright of every believer in Jesus Christ!

It is true that not every believer has claimed his birthright, but it is his, promised by God and provided by God, through a crucified, risen and ascended Saviour. If you have not claimed your birthright, it is your own fault, but you may claim it today.

There rests upon us a solemn obligation to be baptized with the Holy Spirit. It is not merely a matter of privilege; it is a matter of duty. If we pay the price for this blessing, it will be ours, and souls will be won to Christ, who will not be won, if we do not pay the price, and therefore do not obtain the blessing.

If we do not pay the price and do not obtain the blessing, we will be responsible before the Lord for everyone that might have been saved, who was not saved, because we did not pay the price, and therefore, did not obtain the blessing.

I often tremble for myself and for others who are in the ministry. And, by the ministry, I do not mean merely the ministry as ordinarily defined, as including only ordained ministers. But, I use it in the broader sense, applying to all believers, for we are all called to minister the Gospel in some way.

I say I tremble for myself and for my brethren in the ministry, because there are many who are preaching error. There are many in these days that claim to be preaching the truth, who are preaching in reality, the most pernicious and destructive error, and I tremble for them.

Paul said in **2 Timothy 4:2-4, "Preach the word; be instant in season, out of season; reprove, rebuke, exhort with all long-suffering and doctrine. For the time will come when they will not endure sound doctrine; but after their own lusts shall they heap to themselves teachers, having itching ears; And they shall turn away their ears from the truth, and shall be turned unto fables"**. Here we can see what happens, when those in the ministry preach unsound doctrine. People are turned from the truth because they do not want the truth. They don't want anything that would cause them to live different lives. They are perfectly satisfied living ungodly, fleshly lives without any cause for conviction.

Paul said in **2 Thessalonians 2:11-12 "And for this cause God shall send them strong delusion, that they should believe a lie: That they all might be damned who believed not the truth, but had pleasure in unrighteousness".** He said they would believe a lie.

It's sad to look in some of our newspapers and see some of the topics that will be preached in our churches. You wonder, where is the truth being preached that will change people's lives? There are sermons about current events, world tragedies and topics to make you laugh and feel good. But, where are the messages that declare, "Thus saith the Word of the Lord".

I tremble for those who are preaching the Gospel - preaching the Gospel in its simplicity, in its purity and in its fullness. Preaching it as Paul states in **1 Corinthians 2:4 "And my speech and my preaching was not with enticing words of man's wisdom, but in demonstration of the Spirit and of power".**

It's not enough that we preach the Gospel, not enough that we preach it in its simplicity; its purity, its fullness, but we must preach it in the power of the Holy Spirit. **2 Corinthians 3:6 "Who also hath made us able ministers of the new testament; not of the letter, but of the spirit: for the letter killeth, but the spirit giveth life". We can do this only as we are definitely baptized with the Holy Spirit!**

STUDY QUESTIONS FOR CHAPTER THREE

What was necessary for the disciples to do the work the Lord had called them to do and how were they to receive it?

What two Scriptures are used to explain the Baptism with the Holy Spirit?

What course did the disciples take to prepare them for their work and who was their teacher?

What is the literal meaning of the word "tarry"?

What two questions should be asked of those graduating from Bible college or university before we ordain them?

What Scripture explains how Jesus received the power of the Holy Spirit, and where was He when He received it?

What are the Scriptural references for us receiving a refilling of the Holy Spirit?

Give the Scriptures to prove you can have the Baptism with the Holy Spirit.

What are the different interpretations of the "promise" in Acts 2:39? Which of the two is correct?

What are two different laws of interpretation? Explain the different laws.

To whom is the "promise" given? Are we included? If so, how are we included?

What is our solemn obligation as a believer? Are we responsible for the salvation of others?

What happens if ministers preach unsound doctrine? What Scripture is used to verify what happens?

What did Paul say was more important than his speaking ability and his wisdom?

CHAPTER FOUR

This is That

What an exciting day for the early church! **"And there appeared unto them cloven tongues like as of fire, and it sat upon each of them. And they were all filled with the Holy Ghost and began to speak with other tongues, as the Spirit gave them utterance." Act 2:3,4**. The Lord had given what He had promised. **"And, behold, I send the promise of my Father upon you: but tarry ye in the city of Jerusalem, until ye are endued with power from on high." Luke 24:49**. These 120 who were fearful, uncertain of their future, and hiding behind closed doors for fear of the Jews, were now endued with power from on high and, ready to accomplish the task before them. What had happened to change them? **They had been baptized with the Holy Spirit!**

The greatest day since the birth, death and resurrection of our wonderful Lord was dawning. Those 120 were filled with joy. They were speaking in other tongues. Those who were gathered were all amazed at what was happening and asked, **"What meanest this?"** Peter had an answer for the mocking, doubting, bewildered crowd that asked the meaning of the Pentecostal phenomenon. He said, **"But this is that which was spoken by the prophet Joel; And it shall come to pass in the last days, saith God, I will pour out of my Spirit upon all flesh: —" Acts 2: 16,17**.

The Holy Spirit, which had fallen upon them, would now begin guiding and directing. This happens when we are filled with the

Holy Spirit. He becomes our guide. He leads us. He directs our paths. And, oh, how the church world needs the fullness of the Holy Spirit today.

The Pentecostal movement emphatically asserts that the Baptism of the Holy Spirit can be the experience of every sincere born-again believer today! I believe the message and teaching on the Holy Spirit is one of the most prominent themes in the New Testament. Let us see what the Scriptures have to say about it.

THIS IS THAT WHICH WAS PROPHESIED BY JOEL.

Joel, the prophet, writing the words 795-755 B.C., but now quoted here by Peter, declared that the Holy Spirit would be poured out upon **all flesh.** What a tremendous statement! **Poured out upon all flesh!** It does not matter how old you may be. It does not matter how young a child may be, if that child can, by faith, believe.

I was preaching a revival several years ago at First Assembly of God in Venice, Florida when one evening an elder gentleman came forward to seek for the Baptism of the Holy Spirit. It was evident he was crippled. I found out later that he had rheumatoid arthritis and had been crippled for years. He responded that evening to the invitation to receive the Baptism of the Holy Spirit. I began praying with him to receive the Baptism. It was not long until suddenly he burst out speaking in tongues. But, when he was filled with the Holy Spirit, the Lord also healed him! He began dancing in the Spirit back and forth across the front of the church, speaking in tongues. All heaven came down in the service. He danced back to where I was standing and suddenly picked me up and began spinning around, still talking in tongues. I found out that the man was **ninety-one years old!!** The Lord had not only filled him with the Holy Spirit, but had healed him as well, at ninety-one years of age. Joel, and Peter, quoting Joel, said,' **I will pour out of my Spirit upon all flesh**..."

A few years after this experience, I was preaching a revival in Fresno, California. We were having a number of people receiving the Baptism, when one evening an Hispanic gentleman came forward to seek for the infilling of the Holy Spirit. He had been raised in a denomination that did not believe in speaking in other tongues. But, he was hungry to receive everything the Lord had for him. When he came forward his little boy also came with him. His son put his arms around his dad's leg and held on tightly. As I was praying with the man, giving him instructions on how to yield to the Holy Spirit, his son would lean back and look up at his dad. You could tell he had never seen his dad do anything like that before. It wasn't but just a few minutes until his dad was filled with the Holy Spirit and began speaking in tongues. You should have seen the look on his son's face. He leaned back and looked up at his dad with eyes opened wide. I knelt down beside him and asked if he would like to receive what his dad had just received. He said, 'uh huh.' I asked him to raise his hand and begin praising the Lord like his dad had done. And, in simple child like faith, he began praising the Lord. It wasn't but just a few minutes until he burst out speaking in tongues. I heard a sound behind me as the pastor had suddenly taken off running and praising the Lord. When he returned, he asked me if I had any idea how old the little boy was. I told him I had no idea. He told me the boy was only **four years old**! **This is that spoken of by the prophet Joel!**

He will pour out the Holy Spirit upon **all** men, or women, bond or free. He will pour it out upon **any denomination**. It doesn't matter if you are Baptist, Methodist, Lutheran, Presbyterian, Catholic or Pentecostal. He will pour out His blessed Holy Spirit upon every hungry waiting heart.

In Old Testament times, only special people had an anointing of the Holy Spirit. All the gifts of the Spirit, with the exception of the gift of tongues and interpretation of tongues were evident in their lives.

But, today, **all** can be Spirit-filled, endued with power, baptized with the perpetual indwelling of the Holy Spirit!

THIS IS THAT PREDICTED BY JOHN THE BAPTIST

John stated in **Matthew 3:11 "I indeed baptize you with water unto repentance: but he that cometh after me is mightier than I, whose shoes I am not worthy to bear: he shall baptize you with the Holy Ghost, and with fire."** John's baptism was outwardly symbolical of an inward cleansing.

The Baptism of the Holy Spirit is an **inward infilling.** John stated it is a **baptism of fire!** So, when we are filled with the Holy Spirit, the fire of the Spirit will begin burning within us. And, as is the case with any fire, it will consume anything that is dead and dry. There are those all around us who are **"...dead in trespasses and sin." (Ephesians 2:1)**

The Baptism of the Holy Spirit is the **outward evidence of an inward infilling.** Jesus said, **"...out of his belly shall flow rivers of living water. But this spake he of the Spirit, which they that believe on him should receive..." (John 7:38,39)** When that river begins flowing and you begin speaking in other tongues, the outward sign that you have been filled, is **"...cloven tongues like as of fire that sat upon each of them." (Acts 2:3)** When you receive the Holy Spirit, there is suppose to be a fire burning within your soul!! That fire will not only consume you, but will consume those who are dead and dry around you.

Another characteristic of the fire of the Spirit is that it **spreads!** When a fire begins, it will spread quickly across a field of dry grass, or race through a forest. It spreads in all directions.

Fire attracts attention! People love to see a fire. They will follow a fire truck to find what is burning. And, I can tell you, let our hearts catch on fire with the Holy Spirit, let our churches catch on fire with the Holy Spirit, and people will come to see what is happening.

I was about fourteen years old when the church in which I was raised had a revival. That revival lasted for four weeks. It was the fourth week of the revival when I gave my heart to the Lord. I also received the Baptism of the Holy Spirit that same week. The night I received the Baptism, four others also received. The five of us young men, my brother, my best friend and his brother, my cousin and I had gone to the altar together. We had tarried and tarried and tarried. I suppose we had tarried, **maybe five minutes**, when I thought that this wasn't to be my night. So, I started to get up, but discovered that we were all hemmed in. The congregation had completely encircled us! That happens after four weeks of revival. Every one wanted us to receive what they had received. So, I knelt back down and started seeking again. It wasn't but just a few more minutes until I received the Baptism and began speaking in other tongues. I was the first of the five to receive. But then, one after the other all received. When the five of us received the Baptism, two sisters in the congregation began singing in tongues. One sang soprano and the other alto. They began singing in tongues, the same language, in perfect harmony. All heaven came down as they sang for more than an hour and a half. They sounded like angels. People were slain in the Spirit without anyone pushing them down. They danced in the Spirit. **The fire of the Holy Spirit was burning!**

Is the fire burning in your heart? Is the fire burning in your church? Begin seeking for a fresh fire to begin in you. If it does, it will spread to your church. And, it will spread to those around you.

You see fire is a symbol of God's presence! The very nature of God is fire. **"For our God is a consuming fire." (Hebrews 12:29**) Look in the Old Testament, when Moses led the children of Israel out of Egypt. A pillar of fire led them by night and a cloud by day. Every time they looked up and saw the fire, they knew the Lord was near. They knew that **"God is our refuge and strength, a very present help in trouble." (Ps.46: 1**) The Lord knew what they needed.

The Lord knows what our needs are today. He knows we need the fullness of the Holy Spirit. He knows we need the Baptism of fire, if we are to reach our generation. When the fire of the Spirit begins burning in our souls, it's evidence that the Lord is with us. When there's no fire and no burning, there will be no spreading. It's time to once again come back to an old-fashion altar and say, "Lord, I want a new touch, and I want a fresh fire, set my soul aflame and burn within me." Oh, John the Baptist predicted it**! "...He shall baptize you with the Holy Ghost, and with fire." (Matt. 3:11)**

THIS IS THAT PROMISED BY JESUS

"For John truly baptized with water; but ye shall be baptized with the Holy Ghost not many days hence."(Acts 1:5) What a tremendous promise Jesus gave! This is God's infallible, immutable, unchanging Word! He said in **Mark 13:31,** **"Heaven and earth shall pass away: but my words shall not pass away."** There's an old song that goes something like this; "every promise in the Book is mine, every chapter, every verse, and every line." Jesus promised the Holy Spirit was coming. In fact, He made a number of outstanding promises.

Jesus promised in **John 14:2,3,"In my Father's house are many mansions: if it were not so, I would have told you. I go to prepare a place for you. And if I go and prepare a place for you, I will come again, and receive you unto myself; that where I am, there ye may be also."** I want to go where Jesus is! That was an outstanding promise that has not yet been fulfilled.

Jesus made another outstanding promise in **John 16:7,** **"Nevertheless I tell you the truth; It is expedient for you that I go away: for if I go not away, the Comforter will not come unto you; but if I depart, I will send him unto you."** He said, **"...I will send him, (referring to the Holy Spirit), unto you."** That promise began on the Day of Pentecost! Jesus said He was not going to leave us comfortless. He was going to send another

Comforter. Then we would have the **dual comfort** of Jesus and the Holy Spirit.

Jesus described the Comforter in **three phases.** In **John 14:17,** **" Even the Spirit of truth; whom the world cannot receive, because it seeth him not, neither knoweth him: but ye know him; for he dwelleth <u>with you</u> and shall be <u>in you.</u>** There's a world today that doesn't see Him, that doesn't know Him, and so, they haven't received Him. But, Jesus said, "...**ye** know him." Oh, **do you know Him?** Do you know, that you know, that you know Him? Why? "For He dwelleth <u>**with you.**</u>"

The Greek word for "dwelleth" is **<u>meno.</u>** It means **" like living together in a tent."** It is like a man and woman who have gotten married, who move into a tent, and they become as one, and stay together in that given place relationship and enjoy the presence of one another.

That's what the Lord said He would do for those who want to be filled with the Holy Spirit. He's going to dwell with us. He's going to come into us, and we're going to dwell together, as a husband and wife, in that long lasting relationship. We're going to walk together, we're going to talk together, and we're going to be together with Him. He has not left us comfortless. He has sent another Comforter that He may abide with us forever!

Then Jesus said, ".... He shall be <u>**in you.**</u>" **(John 14:17).** There is to be within us a river that flows, when He comes in and baptizes us. A river which we can't contain. How long has it been since the Holy Spirit has flowed out of you like a river? How long has it been since that river has overflowed its banks because the Spirit has saturated you?

Can you recall a time when you were so filled, that you were lost in the Spirit or drunk in the Holy Spirit as they were on the Day of Pentecost? Have you ever cried out to the Lord and said, "Lord, hold it just a little bit, I can't hold anymore."? I have been at that place.

A few years ago I was going to preach a revival in Universal City, Texas. As I was driving down I35, south from Oklahoma City, I had put in a tape of our new recording; **"We Love To Tell the Story."** Kenny and Tammy, our son and daughter, had recorded the song, "Jesus Never Fails". I was just south of Waco, when the song began playing. As I listened to the words, I began praising the Lord. The Holy Spirit began flooding my soul. The Holy Spirit flowed like a river. I was crying, talking in tongues, as I praised the Lord. I can recall vividly, asking the Lord to hold it. I didn't feel like I could hold any more. I don't really recall driving the rest of the way to Universal City. I was lost in the Spirit!

Can you recall ever having an experience like that? I can tell you, it is available. **Jesus promised that it was coming**. Now we get so content, and are satisfied with so little, because we have lost the joy, and we've lost the flow. We're empty. We're dry. We've lost the power. We've lost the anointing.

If the Niagara River dried up there would be no Niagara Falls. The falls are there because a river flows. The only way power can be produced is when the river is flowing. When the Holy Spirit has filled us, we will have a river flowing. Why? Because, **"...he dwelleth** with you and shall be **in you."** (John 14:17). And, **"...out of his belly shall flow rivers of living water."** (John 7:38).

Unless there is something within us that continues to supply what we need, we will dry up! And, when we get dry and die spiritually, we will loose the joy and the power and the anointing. Then it becomes an endurance test to see if we can endure until the end. The Lord never intended for it to be an endurance test in our lives. He intended for us to be equipped. He's given us the means whereby we can be equipped. Jesus said, **"For John truly baptized with water; but ye shall be baptized with the Holy Ghost not many days hence."** (Acts 1:5). When we receive the Holy Spirit we're going to be changed! We're going to be different!

The ones to whom He was speaking, could not comprehend

what Jesus was saying to them, when He gave them that promise. He had been with them until that time. But now, He is gone. After the resurrection, after He had ascended back into heaven, no longer were they enjoying His presence. Now, they are living in fear, gathered together behind closed doors.

I see the group, "**.... About an hundred and twenty." (Acts 1:15**), gathered in, "**...an upper room." (Acts 1:13**). They began to pray and prayed about ten days. I don't know how long it may take for us to pray through, but it took them at least ten days. I don't care how long it takes for us to pray through. **It's time for the church to take whatever time is necessary and pray through until the fire begins to fall, and the river begins to flow out of us once again**. That's the plan of God for us! He wants us filled with the power of the Spirit! He wants us witnessing and testifying and loving one another and working together for Him!

He doesn't want us going around, crying out, "Pray for me that I will hold out until the end. The devil has been after me all day long, bless his name!" In so many churches, that is exactly where the congregation is. Instead of being filled with enthusiasm, instead of being endued with power from on high, instead of having a river flowing, we are complacent and lethargic.

Then in **Luke 24:49,"And, behold, I send the promise of my father <u>upon you</u>: but tarry ye in the city of Jerusalem, until ye be endued with power from on high."** The Holy Spirit will mantle us with His love! He will envelop us with His power! He will baptize us with fire! The Lord's plan, for you and me, is that He will be **<u>with</u>** us! He is going to be **<u>in</u>** us! He is going to come **<u>upon</u>** us, so we may be endued with power from on high!

The last promise Jesus gave was **Acts 1:8 "But ye shall receive power, after that the Holy Ghost is come upon you: and ye shall be witnesses unto me both in Jerusalem, and in all Judea, and in Samaria, and unto the uttermost part of the earth."**

THIS IS THAT WHICH PREDOMINATED THE EARLY CHURCH

On the Day of Pentecost, **every waiting member** was filled with the Holy Spirit! Those timid men and women, who entered into that upper room, who had been hiding behind closed doors, suddenly became bold and brave, and turned the then known world upside down.

Peter, who had denied the Lord before the Day of Pentecost, was now filled with the Holy Spirit. Peter, who was boastful and arrogant, claiming, "Lord, I'll never deny you," is now endued with power from on high. The Holy Spirit has come upon Peter and the others in the upper room, and now Peter stands, filled with boldness, filled with power, a river flowing out of him. No longer is he afraid. Peter said in (**Acts 2:22-24**)"**Ye men of Israel, hear these words; Jesus of Nazareth, a man approved of God among you by miracles and wonders and signs, which God did by him in the midst of you, as ye yourselves also know; Him, being delivered by the determinate counsel and foreknowledge of God, ye have taken, and by wicked hands have crucified and slain: Whom God hath raised up, having loosed the pains of death: because it was not possible that he should beholden of it."** When Peter finished his message, three thousand souls were converted. The first recorded invitation in the Bible had been given!

What had made the difference in Peter? **Peter had been filled with the Holy Spirit, with the evidence of speaking in other tongues**. Now, no longer is Peter like a reed blowing in the wind. Peter has become, **" petros,"**, which in the Greek means, **"a fragment of a rock."** Jesus is **" Petra"**, which in the Greek means, **"an immovable stone"**. Christ Himself, is the only foundation of the church. Peter was only one of the builders. He had become a fragment of the Rock.

The Lord wants us to receive the same experience Peter received. He wants us filled with the Holy Spirit, speaking in other tongues. He wants us witnessing and winning souls, just

54

as the early church did beginning on the Day of Pentecost. **(Acts 2:47)"...And the Lord added to the church daily such as should be saved."** His plan now, as it was then, is for us to win souls every day. You say, "but how can I do that?" Get filled with the Holy Spirit and, **"...ye shall receive power, after that the Holy Ghost is come upon you: and ye shall be witnesses unto me..."** (Acts 1:8). Timid men can receive the Baptism of the Holy Spirit and receive the boldness needed to win souls.

Those one hundred and twenty received the Holy Spirit by tarrying approximately ten days. I am afraid it has become a mindset in our Pentecostal churches that that is the only way we can be filled. But, that is not so. However, **tarrying is a way by which you can be filled.**

The Lord sent Peter to the household of Cornelius. Cornelius had had a dream to send for Peter. Peter had had a dream where the Lord sent him to Cornelius's home. And, as Peter preached, **"... the Holy Ghost fell on them that heard the word."** (Acts 10:44) and **"...they heard them speak with tongues, and magnify God."** (Acts 10:46). The household of Cornelius received the Holy Spirit spontaneously as Peter preached. So, **you can receive the Holy Spirit spontaneously as the Word of God is preached.**

When Paul arrived in Ephesus, twenty-six years after the Day of Pentecost, he found disciples who knew nothing about the Holy Spirit. In fact, when he asked them in **Acts 19:2 "... Have ye received the Holy Ghost since ye believed?".** They answered; **"we have not so much as heard whether there be any Holy Ghost." Verse six** states, **"And when Paul had laid his hands upon them, the Holy Ghost came on them; and they spake with tongues, and prophesied."** So, **these received the Holy Spirit by having hands laid on them.**
This is that which predominated the early church. Those people were changed, transformed by the power of God and turned the world upside down. You can see that this was God's plan to

reach the world. God's plan has not changed! He still wants us filled with the Holy Spirit! He wants a river flowing out of us! He wants us endued with power! He wants us baptized in the Holy Spirit, speaking in other tongues as the Spirit gives us utterance, because **He knows the benefits that are ours when we are filled.**

STUDY QUESTIONS FOR CHAPTER FOUR

Explain the following phrases:
      a. "Promise of the Father"
      b. "This is That"   (Acts 2:16,17)
      c. "Endued with power"   (Luke 24:49)
      d. "Poured out on all flesh" (Acts 2:18)
      e. "What meanest this"   (Acts 2)

Explain the statement "Fire is a symbol of God's presence."
(Hebrews 12:29)

Compare John's baptism in Matthew 3:11 with the baptism of
the Holy Ghost and with fire as discussed in Acts 2:3,4.

Name four promises given by Jesus related in :
      a. Acts 1:5
      b. Mark 13:31
      c. John 14:2,3
      d. John 16:7

Identify three phrases used by Jesus in John 14:7 and Luke
24:49 to describe the relationship of the Holy Spirit with spirit-
filled Christians.

What does Acts 1:8 mean to you? Name three ways the
Baptism in the Holy Spirit can make you a more effective witness for Jesus.

Explain the meaning of the following Greek words related to
Peter and Jesus respectively.
      a. Petros
      b. Petra

Briefly relate the story of Cornelius' family receiving the Holy
Spirit in Acts 10:44 and Acts 10:46.

CHAPTER FIVE

These Signs Shall Follow Them That Believe

God has given us something wonderful in Pentecost!!

You see, <u>**the distinguishing feature of Pentecostal people is not that they believe in the Lord's soon return!**</u> There are many other denominations that believe in the Lord's return.

<u>**We are not unique because we believe in the Lord's healing power!**</u> There are many other denominations that practice regularly the laying on of hands for the sick to be healed.

<u>**The fact that we believe that there is a Holy Spirit does not make us Pentecostal!**</u> You can listen to the Apostle's Creed that is quoted on Sunday morning as part of the liturgy in some of the coldest, deadest, old-line churches you have ever seen. They will say, "I believe in God the Father, Almighty, Maker of heaven and earth, and in Jesus Christ, His only Son, our Lord, and then going on a little ways.... And I believe in the Holy Spirit." So, there are many denominations that believe in the Holy Spirit.

<u>**We are not Pentecostal because we believe in the Triune Godhead: God the Father, the Son and the Holy Spirit!**</u>

<u>**We are Pentecostal because we believe in what He does to us**</u>

when we get filled with Him! It is just as simple as that.

God never intended for some people to be Pentecostal and others not to be Pentecostal! It has been His plan from the very beginning that people would be saved and then filled with the Holy Spirit.

Look at the words of Jesus as He gives us the Great Commission in **Mark 16:15-18**. And, by the way, the Great Commission is still for you and me today! Jesus said, **"Go ye into all the world, and preach the gospel to every creature..."** And, that my friends, has never been rescinded. It is just as applicable to us today as it was over two thousand years ago. Then it goes on to say, **"He that believeth and is baptized shall be saved; but he that believeth not shall be damned."** The Great Commission does not end there! It goes on to say, **"And these signs** (now this is not apart from the Great Commission, this is a part of the Great Commission). This is as much a part of the Great Commission as, **"going into all the world and preaching the gospel to every creature."** And, it says, **"And these signs shall follow them that believe;"** if we are believers, then these signs should be following us. They will follow us every day of our lives, every place we go. These signs: **"In my name shall they cast out devils; they shall speak with new tongues"**. And that means exactly what it says, **"new tongues!"**

Did you know that it was God's will that everyone, who is saved, should then be filled with the Holy Spirit? It was God's plan for everyone who made their way to Calvary's hill for the cleansing of the blood, should go from there, to the Upper Room, for the full overflow of the Holy Spirit and power!

When you come to Calvary, Calvary demands a decision! Will you accept the teaching of what happened at Calvary? The fact, that Jesus died and shed His life's blood for you. And, that every drop of His precious blood was for the cleansing of your sins. You have to make a decision about what Jesus did for you and then accept Him as your Lord and Saviour. In so doing, you experience salvation. **Salvation is not a denomination!** Salvation is a personal confrontation with Jesus Christ as Lord and Saviour!

The same thing is true when it comes to the Upper Room! Just as surely as Calvary demands a decision, the Upper Room demands a decision. Will you accept the facts of what happened in the Upper Room? The fact that one hundred and twenty gathered, tarrying for approximately ten days, **"And suddenly there came a sound from heaven as of a rushing mighty wind, and it filled all the house where they were sitting. And there appeared unto them cloven tongues like as of fire and it sat upon each of them. And they were all filled with the Holy Ghost, and began to speak with other tongues, as the Spirit gave them utterance."** Acts 2:2-4. Pentecost had come! But, Pentecost is not a denomination. It, too, is a personal confrontation with Jesus as Baptizer!

There are many people who come into our Pentecostal services to look us over. And, that is all right, because <u>we just love spies</u>! We believe that, what God does, bears looking at! We're not afraid for them to spy out the good things of the Upper Room. But, we urge them; don't just climb the steps and look in. It's better than that. They can have that with which God has so richly blessed us!

A few years ago while preaching a revival in Byesville, Ohio, we had a marvelous miracle on the first Sunday evening. An elderly lady, who had been blind for more than two years, was instantly healed, and received her sight. I had been praying for people to receive the Baptism of the Holy Spirit, and then started praying for those who needed healing. She had come forward for prayer. When I prayed for her, she seemed to float like a leaf and landed on the floor. She just lay there, talking in tongues, for quite a while.

In the mean time, the pastor started having some, which had received the Baptism, give their testimonies. All of a sudden, the lady jumped to her feet and began shouting, "I can see, I can see!" She had been instantly healed! Needless to say, we had camp meeting that night.

Her healing caused quite a stir in the community. It seemed that many people knew her. Every Tuesday her niece would pick her up and take her to the beauty shop. Then she would take her inside and help her hang up her coat. But, on the Tuesday following the miracle, her niece took her to the beauty shop and dropped her off. The little lady walked in to hang up her coat, but they had moved the coat rack to the other side of the shop. So, she walked to where they had moved the coat rack, without any assistance, and hung up her coat. The beauty operator, who always helped her, asked where her niece was. The lady said "I don't need her anymore. The Lord healed me Sunday night and I can see!" It caused quite a commotion in the beauty shop. As a result of the miracle, the meeting was extended.

The following Thursday evening we had a wonderful crowd. I noticed as the service began that there were two distinguished looking gentlemen sitting on the back row. I preached that night on the subject, "But Ye Shall Receive Power, After That The Holy Spirit Is Come Upon You." When I gave the invitation, a number of people came forward. I began praying for them to receive the Baptism and many began receiving. I noticed that the two men, who had been seated on the back row, had come forward to see what was happening in the altar service. One of the men motioned with his finger for me to come back to where they were standing. I told him I was busy praying for people and that he would have to come to me. The two men made their way through the crowd and came and stood in front of me. One of them leaned over and whispered, "We are pastors of another denomination from the area. We have heard what happened Sunday night when the little old lady was healed, and we have come to see for ourselves what is happening. You have just preached on," receiving power after the Holy Spirit is come upon you." We don't have that power. Do you think the Lord will give us that power?"

I told them that if they were hungry, and wanted to receive, that they could. They both said they wanted to receive. I told them to raise their hands and begin praising the Lord. It was not but just a few minutes until they both burst out speaking in tongues, as they too, received the Holy Spirit. They had come that night as, "spies." But, they left endued with power from on high. That experience made a tremendous impact in the community.

Now notice what Jesus said in **Mark 16:17, "...they shall speak with NEW tongues"**. The word "new" here has two separate meanings at this point.

The **first meaning** for the word **"new"** means: **"with a tongue refreshed and made over."** There are a lot of people in our churches who need the Baptism: Amen?

I mean, **"these signs shall follow them that believe."** I believe you need to believe for a new tongue as well. Now, I am not talking about another language. I'm talking about this tongue of ours being made over, and having it refreshed and made brand new.

You see Pentecostal people are not supposed to talk like other people talk! It's not enough to have the **"Pentecostal"** label on the lamp. You had better have the Pentecostal oil on the inside as well. There are some people who carry the label on the outside of the lamp, who have long since run out of the oil, and they have gone back to talking the way they use to talk. You can always tell when the oil runs out! People become critical, self-centered and judgmental.

Gretnia and I were preaching a revival out in the northwestern part of Oklahoma several years ago. One night after the service, the pastor's wife told her husband of a strange phone call she had had that day. It seems she had picked up the phone to make a call and discovered she could hear two women from their church conversing. The women did not know the pastor's wife was on the phone and could hear their conversation. The women were being critical and talking about different people in the church. When they finished their conversation, the pastor's wife called the ladies and told them that it was absolutely terrible what they were saying about people in their church. She said, "You need to ask the Lord to forgive you, and then ask the people about whom you have been talking to forgive you, and then stop talking about people!" You can always tell when the oil runs out! By the way, those ladies thought the pastor's wife had the Gift of the Word of Knowledge!

We need to stay **FULL, FULL, FULL** of the Holy Spirit! If we do, our nature's going to be sweet. We will lift up others. We will encourage each other. We will bless them. We won't criticize them. If there is something about which we're critical, we won't go to each other. We will take it to Jesus and cry out to Him and ask Him to do the work and speak to hearts. We're not the ones He has commissioned to do that. He must do the work. So, you can always tell when people have run out of oil. They need a **"new"** tongue!

The **second meaning** for the word **"new"** here in the Greek means: **"languages."** They shall speak with new tongues, new **"languages'** they've never learned. There are a lot of people who say, "Well, I like that first one, but I'm not sure about that second one!" Well, both of the meanings are there. I didn't write it, I'm just sharing it with you. They shall speak with **"languages"** that they never knew before.

Jesus was laying the foundation for what was getting ready to happen on the Day of Pentecost. He had told His disciples in **Luke 24:49**, **"...but tarry ye in the city of Jerusalem, until ye be endued with power from on high."**

Now, I want you to understand something here. Those men, to whom He made that statement, had already experienced a great deal of power. Jesus had commissioned them in **Luke 10:9**, to **" . . . heal the sick that are therein, and say unto them, The kingdom of God is come nigh unto you." Verse 17** stated,

"...they returned again with joy, saying, Lord, even the devils are subject unto us through thy name." But, Jesus said in verse 20, **"Notwithstanding in this rejoice not, that the spirits are subject unto you; but rather rejoice, because your names are written in heaven."**

So, they had the power. But, what Jesus was talking about, was more power than what they had experienced, up until this time, in their lives. They shall speak with languages they never learned. They shall be endued with power from on high. Again, **Mark 16:17,18," And these signs shall follow them that believe; In my name shall they cast out devils; they shall speak with new tongues; They shall take up serpents; and if they drink any deadly thing, it shall not hurt them; they shall lay hands on the sick, and they shall recover."**

Explain the statement "We are Pentecostal because we believe in what He (Holy Spirit) does to us when we are filled with Him! It is as simple as that."

In Mark 16:15-18 Jesus gives us what is known as the Great Commission. Share your thoughts on the following:

      a. "Go ye into all the world and preach the Gospel to every creature."

      b. "He that believeth and is baptized shall be saved, but he that believeth not shall be damned."

      c. "And these signs..."

      d. "In my name shall they cast out devils; they shall speak with new tongues."

Explain the comment, "I believe you need to believe for a new tongue as well." What are the two different meanings of the term new tongues.

Is it possible for the oil of the Holy Spirit to become used up or run out? Give several reasons for your answer.

CHAPTER SIX

The Benefit of Speaking in Tongues

Notice to whom **1 Corinthians** is written "Unto the church of God which is at Corinth, to them that are sanctified in Christ Jesus, called to be saints, **with all that in every place call upon the name of Jesus Christ our Lord**, both theirs and ours." **(I Cor. 1:2).**

Notice, "all that in every place call upon the name of Jesus Christ our Lord," Do people today call upon the name of the Lord? Yes, we do! So, what is written in this book of I Corinthians, is still for us today! **"Jesus Christ the same yesterday, and to day, and for ever." (Hebrews 13:8).**

1 Corinthians 14 is part of the book that is written to, **"all that in every place call upon the name of Jesus Christ our Lord.".** This is probably one of the most misunderstood chapters in the Bible. It deals with the subject of **speaking in other tongues.** There are **two ways** to speak in tongues dealt with in the chapter. We will deal with both of them. The **first,** is our receiving the Holy Spirit, and, tongues are the initial evidence that we have been filled. The **second,** is the Gift of Tongues, which is one of the nine gifts of the Spirit.

There are some people who take a violent stand against speaking in tongues. They are so opposed that they claim it's satanic or of the devil. When people make that statement to me, I smile and say, "give me chapter and verse please." And, they can't. It isn't in the Book! For, if what they have said is true, then, **2**

Cor. 13:1 is not true. "...In the mouth of **two or three** witnesses shall every word be established.". **There is not one Scripture, which says that speaking in tongues is of the devil!**
When they can't give me Scriptures, then I ask them to turn with me to **Rev. 22:18,19** "For I testify unto every man that heareth the words of the prophecy of this book, If any man shall **add unto these things**, God shall **add unto him the plagues that are written in this book;** And if any man shall **take away** from the words of the book of this prophecy **God shall take away his part out of the book of life**, and out of the holy city, and from the things which are written in this book.".

I don't know what people do with the latter part of the verse. There are those who believe once you are saved, your name can't be removed. This verse refutes that belief!

It is serious business, attributing to the devil, what is actually from the Lord. This has been the devil's plan from the beginning. He wants to keep us from being filled with the Holy Spirit. So, he says, "Speaking in tongues is of the devil; speaking in tongues died away when the apostles passed off the scene; speaking in tongues is not necessary today". **God never said that!** Those are the devil's lies!

The Lord did say in **Acts 2:39,** "For the promise is **unto you**, and **to your children**, and to **all that are afar off, even as many as the Lord our God shall call**". The Lord has never stopped calling! The promise is still for us today!

Speaking in tongues were **never** meant to be **controversial or argumentative**! It has always been God's plan for us to be saved and then be filled with the Holy Spirit, so we can win souls and reach a lost and dying world with the gospel!

We don't receive the Baptism of the Holy Spirit so we can have do-daddies run up and down our spines! We don't receive the Holy Spirit so we can run faster, shout louder or jump higher! We receive the Holy Spirit to become **soul winners!** And, that's the reason the devil does everything he can to keep us from being filled.

When it comes to the subject of speaking in other tongues as the Spirit gives utterance, we have people who use the Word of God on this particular subject, in a completely different way from what they would use the Word of God on any other subject. If they were to clip, and cut out, and cast aside, and reject the Scriptures on **salvation** the way they reject the Scriptures on **speaking in tongues**, no one would ever be saved!

In the book of 1 **Corinthians**, we have the **tongues chapter**. In the Bible there are great chapters which deal with great subjects.

1 Corinthians 13 is the **"Love"** chapter!
Hebrews 11 is the **"Faith"** chapter!
Isaiah 53 is the **"Salvation"** chapter!
1 Corinthians 14 is the **"Tongues"** chapter!

Something wonderful happens when we are filled with the Holy Spirit, with the evidence of speaking in other tongues. I want us to look at **1 Corinthians 14,** the **"tongues chapter",** and the subject, **"What's The Benefit of Speaking in Other Tongues".**

BENEFIT ONE: SPEAKING TO GOD

Benefit number one is found in **1 Corinthians 14:2, "For he that speaketh in an unknown tongue speaketh not unto men, but unto God;".**

What do we call it when we are talking to God? **Prayer....** It's just that simple. If there were something wrong with speaking in other tongues, it could not possibly be called, "speaking unto God". Why speak to Him if He doesn't hear us? Why speak to Him if He is displeased with how we're doing it? When we are filled with the Holy Spirit and begin speaking in other tongues, we're not speaking to man; we're speaking **directly to the Father!**

This is not "**the** " way to pray, but it becomes "**another**" way to pray!

One of the most difficult things that we face, as Christians, is "How can we have an adequate life of communications with the Lord"? The devil fights us every way he can to keep us from communicating and talking with the Lord. Have you ever noticed when you begin praying everything seems to happen? Your neck begins to hurt, your back aches, and the phone rings, the kids start fighting. Why? The devil doesn't want us talking to the Lord. If he can keep us from talking to the Lord, he will keep us from a lot of answered prayer.

God has given us the means whereby we can communicate directly with Him. When we are filled with the Holy Spirit and begin speaking in other tongues, we begin immediately communicating with Him. He is the goal of what we are speaking. We're not talking to man.

I've had people come to me and say," Oh, Brother McGee, it is so confusing when everyone begins speaking in tongues at once in our services". **To whom is it confusing?** It may be confusing to man, but **it's not to God**! People may say, "Well, I can't understand a thing they're saying". Well, we're not talking to you. We're talking to God! I've told people many times, " I don't care if you like the way I'm talking in tongues or not. I'm not talking to you; I'm talking to God"!

On the Day of Pentecost, all 120 spoke in tongues at the same time and it was perfectly in order! Why? Because they were not speaking to each other, they were speaking to God.

I wonder what would happen in our churches, if we would get together and pray for ten days? What would happen in our individual lives, if we shut ourselves in with Him, and prayed ten days? Would there be " a sound from heaven as of a rushing mighty wind " filling our churches and individual hearts? I pray, "Oh, Lord, let us feel the breath of God breathing upon us once again. Let the wind of the Spirit come, sweeping across our churches and lives". **Do it again Lord, do it again!**

"Cloven tongues like as of fire, sat upon each of them". The word **"cloven"**, here in the Greek, meant, **"tongues parting asunder, tongues moving a different way"**. They were talking to God in a heavenly language! Can you imagine what they were thinking as they heard each other speaking such strange things? They had never seen or heard any thing like this before in their lives! These **"cloven"** tongues were a sign to unbelievers! That is what Paul said in **1 Corinthians 14:22, "Wherefore tongues are for a sign, not to them that believe, but to them that believe not;".**

They knew they were not speaking to each other, because they could not understand what was being said. **They were speaking to God! God was the goal!** They were communicating directly with their heavenly Father. They were speaking languages they had never learned. They were having camp meeting! They were excited about what was happening!

It must have been quite a scene that day, as those 120 staggered out of the upper room. They must have been weaving and acting as though they were drunk, because people began mocking them and saying, **"These men are full of new wine". Acts 2:13.**

My prayer is that we get so full of the Holy Spirit, speaking in other tongues as the Spirit gives us utterance, that people will think that we are drunk on the Spirit!

After I had received the Baptism as a teenager, my life was so different, that my school friends began calling me a " **Holy Roller**". That made me mad until I found out what "**Holy Roller**" meant. I went to the third addition of Webster's dictionary to find out what it meant. Webster defines a "**Holy Roller**" as, **"a religious sect who becomes so full that they cannot contain themselves, and they give way to their emotions".** Oh, give us more "**holy rollers**".

Isn't it marvelous that God has given us a means, by the Holy Spirit, whereby we can talk to the Lord! This is what praying in other tongues is all about. **1 Corinthians 14:2, "For he that speaketh in an unknown tongue speaketh not unto men, but unto God".** You can see immediately, that by the Spirit, out of the heart of the believer, in a language he has never learned, by a miracle, there is poured heavenward, words you never learned, and **God is the goal!** This is experienced only by the Spirit-Filled!

BENEFIT TWO: HE SPEAKETH MYSTERIES

Benefit number two is also found in **1 Corinthians 14:2**, "…. howbeit in the spirit **he speaketh mysteries**". The Greek word for "**mysteries**" is "**musterion**", which means, "**secret things**".

It always bothers me to hear someone going around, telling everyone, everything that he says to the Lord and, what the Lord says to him! I think there are some things so treasured, so precious, just between me and the Lover of my soul that others should not know.

There are some that feel that they have to ask the Lord for everything. They won't take a bite of food until they get clearance from heaven! God built me so that I know when it's time to eat.

You don't have to ask the Lord if it's time to go to bed. When it gets late and you don't go to bed, you have problems. God made us, so that when we get tired, we know its time to lie down. These things are not secret things.

But, there are some things that are absolutely beautiful, that can only pass between us and God, and God and us!

"**He that speaketh in an unknown tongue**", speaks secret, divine, mysterious things **to God**! Hallelujah!!

Now would you like to get happy? Real happy? I know there are a lot of people who could use some happiness in their lives.

If the devil knew what was going on, when you are communing with God in other tongues, it wouldn't be a secret thing!! But the Holy Spirit said, "For he that speaketh in an unknown tongue speaketh not unto men, but **unto God**", **1 Corinthians 14:2.** We're speaking secret things **to God** when we are speaking in tongues!

The devil wants in on all our prayers and petitions to the Lord. **I think we should make the devil as lonely as we possibly can**. Get full of the Holy Spirit! Pray in the Spirit! We do not pray in other tongues to shut the devil out, because that is automatic! I want you to see the importance of praying in the Spirit.

In the **tenth chapter of Daniel.** Daniel had set his face to seek God. **Verse three** states Daniel, **"...ate no pleasant bread, neither came flesh nor wine in my mouth, neither did I anoint myself at all, till three whole weeks were fulfilled".** This is a long time for a man to be in fasting, prayer, and constant emotional strain.

He had waited and waited and waited for the answer to come. Twenty one days passed. And finally, Gabriel comes and says in **verse 12** "...Fear not, Daniel: for from the **first day** that thou didst set thine heart to understand, and to chasten thyself before thy God, **thy words were heard, and I am come for thy words".** He said," Daniel, from the very first day you set your face to seek God, God heard you, and He gave me the answer. I started back with the answer, **"but the Prince of the kingdom of Persia withstood me one and twenty days" Daniel 10:13.** The battle became so intense I had to call for **"Michael, one of the chief princes, who came to help me" verse 13."**

Ephesians 2:2 tells us that Satan is **"...the prince of the power of the air...".** He is the prince of the power of the air for the first heaven and the second heaven, but not the third heaven.

Isaiah 14:12-14 "How art thou fallen from heaven, O Lucifer, son of the morning! how art thou cut down to the ground, which didst weaken the nations! For thou hast said in thine heart, I will ascend into heaven, I will exalt my throne above the stars of God: I will sit also upon the mount of the congregation, in the sides of the north: I will ascend above the heights of the clouds; I will be like the most High". God had dispatched from the portals of glory, which is the third heaven, the answer to Daniel. Gabriel was commissioned to bring the answer. As he descends from the third heaven, he runs into **"the prince of the powers of the air",** and a battle royal begins. The battle is so great that he has to call for Michael to help him. They fight Satan for twenty-one days, but finally the answer comes.

Satan attempted to keep the answer from coming because he knew what the petition was. **He knows what our petitions are!** I want you to put yourself in the devil's place for just a moment. If you were the devil, would you want every Christian's prayer to be answered? If Satan allowed every prayer to be answered, what chance would he have of getting us back to serving him? He wouldn't have a chance! So, he wants to hinder our prayers. If he can cause us to doubt that our prayers are going to be answered, he has a chance. When our answers are delayed, even though it is the devil's fault, because he is fighting to keep them from being answered, we begin wondering if the Lord heard our prayer. We begin feeling the Lord doesn't really care or maybe He isn't interested in our needs. **That is a lie directly from the pit of hell!** God does care! He is interested! He is concerned! It is just the devil hindering our prayers from being answered.

The Lord knew from the beginning that the devil would attempt to discourage us in this manner. So, He gives us a means whereby we can get our prayers answered, **without the devil knowing** what the petitions are! Again, **1 Corinthians 14:2** "For he that speaketh in an unknown tongue speaketh not unto men, but **unto God**;...howbeit in the spirit he speaketh **mysteries**".

When we are filled with the Holy Spirit, we begin praying in the Spirit. The Spirit helps us, as we are told in **Romans 8:26,27 "Likewise the Spirit also helpeth our infirmities: for we know not what we should pray for as we ought: but the Spirit itself maketh intercession for us with groanings which cannot be uttered. And he that searcheth the hearts knoweth what is the mind of the Spirit, because he maketh intercession for the saints according to the will of God"**.

The Holy Spirit comes in and begins to formulate through us , in our prayer language, the petitions going directly to the throne of God. It does not matter if the devil is standing at the throne, as we see him pictured in the first chapter of Job. He comes as the accuser , as he did against Job. But, he will have to stand and shake his dirty head and wonder what is being said. When you are praying in the Holy Spirit, you're praying secret things, directly to the Father. The Father receives the petition and sends back the answer. The devil doesn't know what the petition is and he doesn't know the answer. He doesn't know when it is going to be sent. So, **we can have our needs met and our prayers answered because we're praying in the Holy Spirit**!

No wonder the devils says, "Now don't get too excited about this Holy Spirit business. It isn't necessary to talk in tongues".

What's the benefit of speaking in other tongues? Because, when you're filled with the Holy Spirit and you're speaking in other tongues, you're speaking directly **to the Father**. He's the object of your conversation. **The second benefit**: you're speaking secret things **to God.**

I know there are those who say, "Well, the devil can understand all the languages of the earth, because he's the prince of the powers of the air. How can he not understand when you are talking in tongues"?

There was a time in eternity past when Satan was cast out of heaven. He was just a created angel. **He is not a member of** the Triune Godhead! He is **not omniscient**! He is **not omnipotent**! He is **not omnipresent**! He **is limited in his power and ability**! God only allowed him to go so far with Job. When we are filled with the Holy Spirit and begin speaking in other tongues, **we are speaking a heavenly language**. A language given to us **by the Lord, "...he shall baptize you with the Holy Ghost, and with fire", Matt. 3:11,** but communicated through us by the Holy Spirit! We simply become the channel through which the Holy Spirit can flow. He is speaking through us, directly to the Father, secret things that the devil cannot understand, **because it is communication between members of the Godhead**! It was the **Holy Spirit**, speaking through Paul in **1Corinthians 14:2**, who said, "...howbeit in the spirit he speaketh **mysteries (secret things)**".

Now there are times when you speak in tongues and you are understood! You speak in tongues and it is a sign **"...to them that believe not", 1 Cor. 14:22.** The devil could understand the earthly language those around you understand. But, that is not the case when you are praying in the Spirit!

The Father, Son and Holy Spirit all want us saved and filled with the Holy Spirit, endued with power from on high, so we can communicate directly with our heavenly Father.

The devil will do anything he can to keep us from receiving the Holy Spirit. Several years ago, in one of our churches, was a lady who had taken it upon herself to keep the church clean. After the evening services were over, she would pick up all the paper and gum wrappers. She felt that was her ministry for the Lord. The lady did not have the Holy Spirit. She would come forward each evening seeking the Baptism. She would praise and worship the Lord and get so close to receiving the Baptism, then suddenly get up and go back to her seat.

One evening, after she had gone back to her seat, one of the ladies from the church sat down beside her and asked if she really wanted to receive the Baptism. The lady answered, "Oh, yes, but I'd rather receive it when I am here by myself". Her friend asked, "Why, would you want to be here by yourself"? The lady turned to her and asked, "do you promise you won't tell anyone"? The friend assured her she would not. She said, "You see I wear "**uppers**", and I'm afraid if I get the Holy Spirit, I'll lose my "**uppers**".

Now that is terrible information to have, that you cannot share with anyone! But the lady from the church said she would not tell anyone. She did call several ladies from the church and asked them to fast and pray that this lady would receive the Baptism the next night.

When the invitation was given the next night for those who wanted to receive the Holy Spirit, the lady came forward as she had done each night before. And, as she had done the previous services, she knelt and prayed with her head down. But, suddenly, she threw her hands up and her head back and shouted, "**Well, let 'em flip!**". When she did, the Holy Spirit fell on her and she began speaking in tongues. But, **she didn't lose her "uppers"**. The devil had used that fear to keep her from receiving the Baptism.

What fear do you have? Why are you not seeking the Holy Spirit? Is it a fear of losing your wig, or maybe your toupee? Are you afraid your make-up may be messed up? Are you afraid you may lose you eyelashes? The Holy Spirit will **never** do anything of which you will be ashamed! **Don't let the devil rob you of a great blessing!**

The devil knows the benefits of you being filled with the Holy Spirit, speaking in other tongues. He doesn't want you speaking **directly to God**. He doesn't want you speaking **secret things to God**.

BENEFIT THREE - HE EDIFIETH HIMSELF

Benefit number three is found in **1 Corinthians 14:4** "He that speaketh in an unknown tongue **edifieth himself**...".

Some people say that Pentecostals act **"puffed-up"**; that we act like we're better than anyone else. Well, we're not better than anyone else; we're just better than we were! Our big problem **is not,** "how can I get better than someone else"? Our problem **is** how can I get better than I was?

When you receive the Baptism of the Holy Spirit, He will enhance every area of you life. Your **spirit** will be revived! Your **soul** will be refreshed! The Holy Spirit will illuminate your mind! The Spirit of God will invigorate your body as He flows through you!

It will even get into your pocket book when you get filled with the Holy Spirit! You will never question if it is God's will to pay tithes. When you get full of the Holy Spirit, the Holy Spirit will bring the Word of God to your remembrance. The Holy Spirit is our teacher and the Word of God says the tithe is the Lord's. **Leviticus 27:30 "and all the tithe of the land, whether of the seed of the land, or of the fruit of the tree, is the Lord's: it is holy unto the Lord".** We will give to the Lord what is rightfully His!

The tithe is not ours to do with what we want to do! We don't use the tithe to buy a more expensive home, or a better car, or a bigger boat or the latest and best **"hell-a-vision"** (TV). You don't take trips and vacations using the Lord's money!

It's important that we be obedient in our tithing! A question is asked in **Malachi 3:8 "Will a man rob God? Yet ye have robbed me. But ye say Wherein have we robbed thee? In tithes and offerings".** God says we rob Him if we don't give Him our tithes. He went even further in **verse 9 "ye are cursed with a curse, for ye have robbed me, even this whole nation".** If we don't pay our tithes, we are cursed with a curse! I hope you understand God doesn't bless that which He curses! **If you are not tithing, you are living under a curse of**

God! Now don't get mad at me, because I didn't say that. This is what God's Word says!

Notice what God's Word states in **1 Corinthians 6:9,10** "Know ye not that the **unrighteous shall not inherit the kingdom of God**? Be not deceived: neither fornicators, nor idolaters, nor adulterers, nor effeminate, nor abusers of themselves with mankind, Nor **thieves,** nor covetous, nor drunkards, nor revilers, nor extortioners, shall inherit the kingdom of God". This is a list of those **not** entering the kingdom of God.

This list names "**thieves.**" If you're **not** tithing; you're robbing God; **you're a thief**! The Lord will have to apologize to every murderer, every homosexual, and every adulterer, if He sends them to hell, and lets people who rob Him of tithes go to heaven!

I imagine those who are not tithers are pretty upset about now. Those who are tithers are saying "sic-em" there may even be a little **"hide- burning"** about now!

When you receive the Baptism of the Holy Spirit, you will fall so in love with Jesus, you will want to give Him everything. You will realize you can't out give God. You will become so liberal, that you want to do everything you possibly can to further the Kingdom of God. You want to support His work. You want to support His people. You want to give the Lord what is rightfully His.

Jesus said in **Mark 12:30** "and thou shalt love the Lord thy God with **all** thy heart, and with **all** thy soul, and with **all** thy mind, and with **all** thy strength...". You get full of the Holy Spirit and He just pours that love into you. You will fall in love with Jesus! You will fall in love with the Father! You will fall in love with the Holy Spirit! You will fall more in love with your companion, your children, and your neighbors. You will even begin loving your enemies! You will love them so much you will want to win them for the Lord! The devil knows that!

The devil doesn't want us winning souls. The devil doesn't want us working for the Lord. He wants to keep us **"under-hungry"** for the Holy Spirit. That's the reason most people aren't filled today. They are **"under-hungry"**. But, Jesus said in **Matthew 5:6** "Blessed (happy) are they which **do** hunger and thirst after righteousness: for they shall be filled".

Let's look at our Scripture again in **1 Corinthians 14:4** "He that speaketh in an unknown tongue edifieth himself...". The word **"edifieth"** has **two major meanings** here in the Greek. The Greek word is **"oikodomeo"**. The first meaning is **"to build"**. You can hear the word "**edifice**" or "**building"** in it! **1 Corinthians 6:19** "What? know ye not that your **body** is the **temple of the Holy Spirit** which is in you, which ye have of God, and ye are not your own?"

This body of ours is the temple of the Holy Spirit. The devil wants to tear this temple down. He wants to wreck us! He wants to vandalize us! I hope you understand the devil doesn't love us. He will do everything he can to destroy this temple of the Holy Spirit. He has one goal for everyone. He wants us to spend eternity, in hell, with him. He wants to destroy our confidence in God. He wants to tear down our faith. He wants to ruin us.

God knew that from the beginning of time. He formulated a plan, where if the devil were to try and destroy this temple (body), He would provide a way to build back what the devil was trying to tear down. **"He that speaketh in an unknown tongue edifieth himself"**. He is "building himself". We're not puffing, magnifying or exalting ourselves, but are building into our being something of a spiritual strength and vitality that is absolutely necessary to carry us through! **When we get full of the Holy Spirit and we're praying in the Spirit, we're building back what the devil is trying to tear down!**

There is a powerful verse in **Jude: 20.** I have it underlined in red in my Bible. I have it colored yellow so the red will stand out! I also have drawn a triangle, which represents a tent, above it, which means: just stop and camp here awhile. It would be good for all to just camp there for a while. **"But ye, beloved, building up yourselves on your most holy faith, praying in the Holy Ghost"**. How do we build ourselves up? **Praying in the Holy Ghost!**

The converse of that statement is also true! If we are not praying in the Holy Spirit, we are allowing ourselves to be torn down! If we're not building, if we're not maintaining, if we're not aggressively trying to build back what the devil is trying to tear down, then just like any building sitting without maintenance, it will begin decaying. This happens in our lives when we cease praying in the Holy Spirit. No longer are we "**building back**", we are allowing ourselves to be torn down!

Several years ago Oklahoma City decided to renovate the downtown area. To do so required a number of buildings be torn down. The demolition of some of the buildings was quite an event. An announcement in the newspaper, on radio and television warned everyone to stay away from those locations the day of their implosion. In the beginning, television crews were on hand, televising the events. We watched, with great excitement, as the countdown began, "10,9,8,7,6,5,4,3,2,1", then **"BOOM"**, and the building would crumble. In less than 30 seconds, the building would be nothing more than a pile of brick and mortar and twisted steel, as dust billowed into the air.

We would say, "Wow, that didn't take long; about 30 seconds"! But, in reality, it had taken a lot longer. Months and months before, engineers began studying the plans of the buildings. They calculated how much of a dynamite charge it would take to destroy the columns of support, and the beams, carrying the weight of the floors. Then dynamite was placed in strategic places, to insure the collapse. Wires would then be run from every charge of explosive to the detonator box. The man in charge would push the plunger and the building was imploded. The building collapsed, only after careful planning and intense detailing to destroy the building had occurred.

The devil wants to destroy our temple! He knows our body is the temple of the Holy Spirit. He knows our weaknesses and our strengths. He has a carefully designed plan to destroy us. He knows what it will take to cause us to crumble. He comes against us, day after day, with temptations, designed to weaken us. Day after day, week after week, month after month we're tempted, and finally, a great temptation comes our way, and **"boom"**, a complete implosion of our temple.

The devil had a plan to destroy Adam and Eve. He used the serpent to beguile Eve. He caused Eve to doubt what God had said. **Genesis 3:1** "...Yea, hath God said, Ye shall not eat of every tree of the garden"? It wasn't long until Adam and Eve partook of the tree of knowledge, and their eyes were opened. They realized they were naked, and sin entered into the world. Satan had laid a snare and it worked. **2 Timothy 2:26** "And that they may recover themselves out of the snare of the devil, who are taken captive by him at his will." We all live with the tragic results of Adam and Eve's fall. They did not have the benefit we have today. We have the privilege of the Baptism of the Holy Spirit, speaking in other tongues, building back what the devil tries to tear down.

The Lord also had a plan. His plan was for us to be filled with the Holy Spirit so we could pray in the Spirit every day. He knew if we prayed in tongues we would build back every thing that the devil would try to tear down. **"He that speaketh in an unknown tongue edifieth himself"**. **He is building himself!**

The second meaning for the word **"edifieth"**, in the Greek, means: **"to make bold".** All of us need more boldness in the Lord! The Lord knew His disciples would need more boldness. He knew we would need more boldness. So, He made provisions for us, just as He did for His disciples.

The Lord told His disciples to go and tarry in the city of Jerusalem until they were "endued with power from on high", because they did not possess the power they needed to do the work the Lord had for them to do. He knew their weaknesses. He knew they would need boldness. He knew they would hide behind closed doors, living in fear. Their source for power was the Baptism of the Holy Spirit. With the Holy Spirit came the boldness they needed.

Before the Day of Pentecost, they were scared. After the Day of Pentecost, they possessed boldness. Before Pentecost, Peter denies he knows his blessed Lord. So vehement was his denial that he begins cursing. Why would he deny his Lord? He denied the Lord because he was so weak. After Pentecost, he stands and preaches, endued with power. What changed Peter? **The Baptism of the Holy Spirit!** No longer is he like a reed blowing in the wind, he has become a rock.

The Lord has given us the means whereby we can have boldness! I'm not talking about being brassy, brash, harsh, brittle or tackless. I'm talking about the ability to say what needs to be said as God anoints us and pours His love through us. There is a great difference between the Spirit-filled who believe for this and for those who don't.

The Holy Spirit gives us boldness that will enable us to take a stand against the devil and any infirmity that he may have put on someone. Boldness that enables us to speak with authority against sickness or disease without worrying that if the healing or deliverance doesn't come, that the people won't believe anything you say from here on. That's a lie the devil passes on to a lot of people! **We should believe what God says!**

This boldness comes by spending much time in pouring your soul out to God in a language the Spirit gives us to pray! **"He that speaketh in an unknown tongue",** is not only building and maintaining himself spiritually, but is at the same time, entering into a life of boldness that otherwise can never be!

It would be wonderful if we could always, spiritually, live on the mountaintop. We all know that is not the case. We all go through valleys and times of testing of our faith.

Several years ago my wife's sister, Loretta Greene, the mother of Tom Greene, who is the current National Youth Director of the General Council of the Assemblies of God, was battling cancer. She had a masectomy, but the cancer had spread to her lungs. Gretnia and I would spend as much time as we could praying for her, even though I was pastor of Faith Tabernacle in Oklahoma City. When we would go to Loretta's house to pray, Gretnia would be on one side of the bed and I would be on the other. As long as we were praying Loretta would be free from pain. As soon as we stopped praying, the pain would begin again. Needless to say, we prayed as much as we could. Our church fasted and prayed for Loretta's healing. The Oklahoma District Council, for whom she had worked as a secretary, prayed diligently. People all over the state of Oklahoma prayed for her healing. People all over the United States, who knew her, prayed for her. All who knew her dearly loved her.

The time came just a few days after her fortieth birthday when she was admitted to St. Anthony's hospital in Oklahoma City. After preaching both services on Sunday, April 28, 1974, I felt the Lord wanted me to stay at the hospital and pray all night for her healing. It was a special time in the presence of the Lord. She deteriorated quickly the next two days. On Tuesday, April 30, one week after her fortieth birthday, the family was called in to be with her during her final hours. As we gathered around her, she suddenly raised her arms and began reaching toward the sky. She evidently could see something or someone we could not see! In just a few moments her arms dropped and she was gone.

At that moment the enemy came and told me I would never pray for anyone else to be healed because my faith was gone. He told me if I didn't have enough faith to pray for my sister-in-law to be healed I would never pray for anyone else to be healed. He did not appear to me in a bodily form. He did not speak in an audible voice. He just spoke to my spirit. When you have been staying up night and day, and you have been fasting and praying, it is easy to get down emotionally and spiritually. Sadly, I listened to him.

I had great difficulty in trying to prepare a message for the following Sunday. I tried to pray, but the heavens seemed to be brass. I would always pray for the sick on Sunday morning, but I did not that Sunday. In fact, I went several Sundays without praying for the sick. Something was wrong because I could not get through to the Lord.

I went to the church on a Monday, after several weeks had passed, and told my secretary I was going to the sanctuary and pray until I received an answer. I told her not to call me unless it was an emergency. I entered the sanctuary and began calling on the Lord. Again, the heavens were brass.

As I was walking and trying to pray, suddenly the Lord spoke to my heart and asked," How long has it been since you praised me? How long has it been since you prayed in the Holy Spirit"? It was as though I had been hit between the eyes with a ball bat! I had gone weeks without praying in tongues! I had gone weeks without praising Him! The devil had been tearing me down. He had been vandalizing me. He had laid a snare for me.

I cried to the Lord and asked Him to forgive me. Then I began praising Him. If I wanted His Presence then I had to praise Him! **Psalms 22:3 "But thou art holy, O thou that inhabitest the praises of Israel".** The word **"inhabitest"** means "the Lord comes to dwell where we are praising Him".

It was not very long until the Holy Spirit flooded my soul. I began praying in the Spirit. It flowed like a river. As I was praying in tongues, the Holy Spirit spoke to my heart and told me to pray for the sick in the following Sunday morning service. I shouted "Yes, Lord, I'll do it"!

The following Sunday morning we had a large crowd. As we were getting ready to begin the service, I looked up and saw a black gentleman entering the sanctuary, being led by Jewel Armstrong, one of our members. I noticed the black man had a red-tipped cane he was carrying, indicating he was blind. The two men were led to seats about halfway down the center isle. Brother Armstrong sent a note to me asking if I would pray for the sick that morning because he had brought his friend who needed prayer for healing.

Immediately, the devil told me I would never pray for anyone to be healed again. Now that is when you need boldness! That boldness comes from praying in the Holy Spirit! **"He that speaketh in an unknown tongue edifieth himself"**! He is **building boldness!** I had heard from heaven that week and I was not about to let the devil keep me from praying for people's needs to be met that morning.

When I received the note, I announced to the church that I would be praying for the sick at the end of the service. I preached and gave the invitation and a number of people came forward for salvation. After I finished the altar call, I then asked for those who wanted prayer for healing to come forward. Again, a number of people came forward for prayer. As they were responding to the invitation, I began lining them up across the front of the church. The black gentleman ended up in the center isle of the church.

Then again, the devil said, "You're going to make a fool of yourself. Your faith is gone." In my spirit, I said, "Devil, I'm not a healer. I'm going to lay hands on the sick and if they are healed, it will be because Jesus has healed them". **Boldness!!**

I must admit, I did not pray for the blind man first. I went to the other end of the line and started praying. The Lord began touching people immediately. As I moved down the line, people were receiving their healing. It was a glorious time!

Finally, I came and stood in front of the black man who was blind. I asked his name? He told me his name was Johnny Jones. I asked how long had he been blind? He told me thirty-six years. I asked him his age? He told me he was seventy-two. I asked why he had come to Faith Tabernacle that morning? He told me he had been praying that week and had felt impressed to call Jewel Armstrong to see if it would be all right to come to our church for prayer. He informed me that he was Baptist and had never been in a Pentecostal church! But, he told me that Brother Armstrong had told him that I prayed for the sick, and he felt he should come for prayer. I asked him if he really believed the Lord could heal him? He told me that was the reason he had come! I asked what had caused his blindness? He told me that he had been working with an acetaline torch and somehow it had slipped in his hand. He said when the torch slipped; the flame had cut across his eyes, blinding him. He told me the doctors had told him he would never see again.

I then asked the church to join with me as I began praying for him. I prayed fervently. I quoted Scripture as I prayed. Then I stepped back and asked him if he could see. He tried to blink his eyes, but he couldn't see. I prayed again. I prayed louder. I quoted more Scriptures. All the time, the devil was telling me I was making a fool of myself. I asked him again if he could see? Again, he tried, blinking his eyes, but to no avail. I told him I had prayed twice: once, in the Name of the Father, once, in the Name of the Son. But this time, I was going to pray in the Name of the Holy Spirit! I then asked the congregation to put their hands over their eyes, as a point of contact, as they joined with me to pray for him.

When I began praying for Johnny, I was praying in tongues. The words flowed like a river. It sounded as though every one in church was praying in the Holy Spirit. When I finished praying, I changed the question I had been asking. I asked Johnny if he could see any light? I'll never forget it as long as I live. He guided his hands and put them on my shoulder and shouted, **"Light? I see you!!"**

And, just like that, the Lord had healed Johnny Jones! I don't have to tell you, but we had camp meeting that morning! People were rejoicing and praising the Lord for the mighty miracle we had witnessed. Our children and young people have never forgotten the creative miracle the Lord performed that day. His story was later written in the history of Faith Tabernacle. Before Johnny left that day, he asked if I would stay at the church until he got home. I did not know at the time what his reason was.

Can you image what his wife thought when he walked out to his car that day. She had dropped him off that morning and left, because it was a Pentecostal church, and she did not want to stay with him. He saw the color of his car for the first time. When she saw him walking to the car, she noticed no one was helping him. When she asked why no one was helping him, he told her he didn't need any help. He said, **"The Lord has healed me"**! They then drove home.

Just a little while later, the phone rang at the church. I answered the phone. Johnny said, "Pastor, I wanted to come home to see if I could still read my Bible. It has been thirty -six years since I have read it." He then began reading the **Twenty-third Psalm, "The Lord is my shepherd..."** Again, there was great rejoicing.

We followed Johnny Jones for the next several years. He retained his sight until he died!!

God had a plan in place for us when we needed it! He knew the enemy would come against us and try to destroy our faith. He knew the devil would try to tear us down and make us weak. So, God gave us the Baptism of the Holy Spirit to help build back the boldness we would need to defeat the devil.

1 Corinthians 14:4 "He that speaketh in an unknown tongue edifieth himself..."

BENEFIT FOUR: I WOULD THAT YE ALL SPAKE WITH TONGUES

1 Corinthians 14:5 "I would that ye all spake with tongues…"

Paul must have been tremendously blessed as he wrote the words given to him by the Holy Spirit. I think that as he wrote, he was saying, "Well, praise God, isn't that wonderful"! When Paul was writing under the influence of the Holy Spirit, what came to him was the Word of God, not the writings of a man named Paul.

So, when you read this, you know that the **Holy Spirit is Pentecostal,** because He says, "I would that ye all spake with tongues".

Jesus had already told his disciples in **Luke 24:49 "And, behold I send the promise of my Father upon you: but tarry ye in the city of Jerusalem, until ye be endued with power from on high".**

He had commanded them to wait until they were endued with power. Had they experienced power up until that time? Yes! **Luke 10:1 "After these things the Lord appointed other seventy also (making 82), and sent them two and two before his face into every city and place, whither he himself would come". And, Luke 10:17 "And the seventy returned again with joy, saying, Lord, even the devils are subject unto us through thy name".**

Did they have the Holy Spirit? **Yes, they had the Holy Spirit, just as everyone who is saved, has the Holy Spirit. In fact, you can't be saved without the Holy Spirit! But**, they were not baptized in the Holy Spirit.

There is a big difference in being filled with the Spirit and being baptized in the Holy Spirit! You can fill a glass half-full with water and say the glass is filled with water. But, the glass is not baptized. It is not filled to the brim and running over, which is what happens when you are baptized.

There are many people in our churches today who profess to be filled with the Spirit, but they do not speak in tongues, because they have not been baptized in the Holy Spirit! They have been saved. They have the Spirit. But, they need to be "endued with power from on high". When you receive the Baptism of the Holy Spirit, with the evidence of speaking in other tongues, you receive that enduement of power from on high according to **Acts 1:8 "But ye shall receive power, after that the Holy Ghost is come upon you..."**

Jesus wanted His disciples to be "filled to the brim and running over ", with the Holy Spirit. So, **we know that Jesus is thoroughly Pentecostal!**

We know the Father is Pentecostal! He says in **Isaiah 28:11 "For with stammering lips and another tongue will he speak to this people"!** You can see the desire of the Father in **Joel 2:28,29 "And it shall come to pass afterward, that I will pour out of my spirit upon all flesh; and your sons and your daughters shall prophesy, your old men shall dream dreams, your young men shall see visions: And also upon the servants and upon the handmaids in those days will I pour out my spirit".** These are the words Peter used to explain what happened on the Day of Pentecost.

The heart-cry of the Father, the Son, and the Holy Spirit is: "I would that ye all spake with tongues..."
The question is: Do you speak in tongues? If not, why? If you do not speak in tongues, it is not because the Father, or the Son, or the Holy Spirit does not want you to. They all want us to be tongue-talking believers!

There are some who would say, "But, the Bible asks in **1 Corinthians 12:30 "...do all speak with tongues?"** inferring that there would be some who do not speak in tongues. Everyone will not speak in tongues because there will always be those who do not want to speak in tongues. **The Baptism of the Holy Spirit is only for those who hunger and thirst after righteousness!**

It is vitally important that we do not take this statement out of its context. Paul is speaking about the Gifts of the Spirit! The verse asks three questions: "Have all the gifts of healing? Do all speak with tongues? Do all interpret?" These are all "Gifts of the Spirit". This is completely different than receiving the Baptism of the Holy Spirit with the evidence of speaking in other tongues. Speaking in other tongues is the initial evidence you have been baptized in the Holy Spirit.

The Gifts of the Spirit are listed in **1 Corinthians 12:8-10 "For to one is given by the Spirit the word of wisdom; to another the word of knowledge by the same Spirit; To another faith by the same Spirit; to another the gifts of healing by the same Spirit; To another the working of miracles; to another prophecy; to another discerning of spirits; to another divers kinds of tongues; to another the interpretation of tongues;" nine gifts in all.**

Paul had mentioned three of the nine. But, he was not saying, some would not speak in tongues if they were baptized in the Holy Spirit! In fact, the opposite was true. he said, "**I would that ye all spake with tongues...**"

People get into trouble in the Word of God, when they take a portion of Scripture out of context, and try to prove a doctrine. Let's leave the Word of God just as the Holy Spirit gave it to Paul: "**I would that ye all spake with tongues...**"

I have had people tell me that tongues cannot be very important because it comes at the end of the list of the Gifts. If you were sent to the store to get milk, eggs, bread and steak; would the steak be less important than the other items? The steak is at the end of the list!

If you want to use that same logic, then look at **1 Corinthians 13:13 "And now abideth faith, hope, charity, these three; but the greatest of these is charity".** What is the greatest of the three? Charity is the greatest, but it's at the end of the list!

Every word, in the Word of God, is given by divine inspiration of the Holy Spirit. All words are equally important. One is not less important than another in the eyes of God.

If we would yield ourselves, everyone could give a message in tongues, everyone could give an interpretation, any of the gifts could operate. **1Corinthians 12:11 "But all these worketh that one and selfsame Spirit, dividing to every man severally as he will".** The Holy Spirit has to have yielded vessels and open channels through which He can flow, for that person to receive the gifts of the Spirit and allow them to operate in and through his life.

There's not a doubt in my mind that the Holy Spirit would love to move and operate in many people's lives that have never yielded themselves to Him! We need a brand new love for everything the Holy Spirit does, and everything He wants in our services. **He wants us yielded to Him, so all the gifts can operate in all our services!**

The gifts most evident in most of our churches are: tongues, interpretation of tongues and prophecy. Where are the other six gifts? The Holy Spirit wants all nine gifts operating! **1 Corinthians 14:26 "How is it then, brethren? When ye come together, every one of you hath a psalm, hath a doctrine, hath a tongue, hath a revelation, and hath an interpretation. Let all things be done unto edifying".**

This is talking about when we come together as a body of believers; that everything is done unto edifying, that the church may be built, that the church be made bold. It is our responsibility, as Spirit-filled believers, to yield ourselves to the Holy Spirit, so all the gifts can operate! The question is: do you yield yourself to Him? He said, **"...when ye come together, every-one of you..."** All of us have a role in every service! Too many are "under-hungry" for the things of God! He said in **Matthew 5:6 "Blessed are they which do hunger and thirst after righteousness: for they shall be filled"**.

The Holy Spirit gave us a plan for an exciting church service! Everyone having a song, a word, a tongue, an interpretation of tongues, a revelation, reveals a flow of the Holy Spirit that is meant to produce excitement. If we were excited about our church services, we would tell everyone! People would come to see what is happening. They would beat a path to our churches!

The Holy Spirit, through Paul, said, **"I would that ye all spake with tongues..."** The Holy Spirit knows the benefit of speaking in tongues! He wants everyone full of the Holy Spirit!

The devil also knows the benefit of us speaking in tongues. That's the reason he works so hard to keep us from doing it. He wants us to remain complacent, and apathetic, and unconcerned. One day, every one of us, from the youngest to the oldest, will stand in His eternal presence and give an account of ourselves. Be willing to be used by God.

Jesus said in **Matthew 7:21 "Not every one that saith unto me, Lord, Lord, shall enter into the kingdom of heaven; but he that doeth the will of my Father which is in heaven"**. What is His will? **"I would that ye all spake with tongues..."**

Each of us does what our master wants us to do! Jesus said in **Matthew 6:24 "No man can serve two masters..."** **Revelation 3:15,16 states: "I know thy works, that thou art neither cold nor hot: I would thou wert cold or hot. So then**

because thou art lukewarm, and neither cold nor hot I will spue thee out of my mouth". I know of no one who stays full of the Holy Spirit that is lukewarm! That's why the Holy Spirit said, "I would that ye all spake with tongues". He knows the benefits that are ours when we are filled with the Holy Spirit! It's time for our churches to cry out to God and say, "Lord, open the windows of heaven and pour your Spirit out upon us"!

It is evident the Lord wants us filled with the Holy Spirit. The question is: **Do we want everyone filled?** I can recall as a young man, when people went to the altar to seek for the Baptism of the Holy Spirit, it seemed the whole church would surround them. It had taken a four-week revival to get people to that place. It takes time to pray and seek the Lord. But, those people prayed until they were full, and then they prayed for those who came, until they were filled. Oh, do it again, Lord!

As I have traveled across the United States, I have found in most of our churches, a real need of people to pray for those who come to the altar. It has been as hard as pulling teeth to get people to pray for one another! It is evident we need a fresh outpouring of the Holy Spirit! If we wanted everyone to speak in tongues, as the Lord wants, we would get filled, and stay full, and pray until it happened.

I was preaching a revival in one of our churches where the Lord was moving. People were being saved and filled with the Holy Spirit. After the Monday evening service, a man came and said he wanted to speak to me. He told me I had made a statement that night in my message he didn't agree with. Well, I have had that happen a lot of times! I asked him with which statement he didn't agree? He said, "You said the initial evidence of receiving the Baptism of the Holy Spirit was speaking in other tongues". He told me he didn't agree with that statement. I felt like I needed to know to whom I was speaking, so I asked him who he was. He informed me he was a deacon in the church. I asked him if he had the Baptism of the Holy Spirit, with the evidence of speaking in other tongues? He told me he did not. I told him if that were the case, he wasn't qualified to be a deacon in an Assemblies of God church! I discovered later there were four deacons in the church who did not believe in speaking in tongues. This was an Assemblies of God church! I cannot tell you how many times I have found this to be true! Not everyone wants everyone to be filled.

I'm afraid there are churches that have popularity contest to choose deacons. They are chosen because they are well known. They are chosen because they give a lot. They are chosen because they have charisma. They should be chosen because they are full of the Holy Spirit, with the evidence of speaking in other tongues, and they meet all other requirements of a deacon.

We experience many problems in our churches because we have lowered the standards. If we desired for all our leaders and workers to be filled with the Holy Spirit, and prayed for it to happen, we might be amazed what the Lord would do.

If God is God, and He wants us filled, if Jesus is Lord, and He wants us filled, if the Holy Spirit is real, and He wants us to speak in tongues, then let's seek Him until that river begins flowing! "I would that ye all spake with tongues".

BENEFIT FIVE: SPEAKING IN TONGUES OPENS OTHER DOORS

1 Corinthians 14:5 "...for greater is he that prophesieth than he that speaketh with tongues, except he interpret, that the church may receive edifying".

Up until this point we have been discussing an individual receiving the Baptism of the Holy Spirit, with the evidence of speaking in other tongues. This is evident in what Paul is saying in **verse two, "For he that speaketh in an unknown tongue speaketh not unto men, but unto God..."** When we are filled with the Holy Spirit, we're speaking directly to God. We're not speaking to man or the church. We are speaking **secret** things to

God, **verse two again, "…howbeit in the spirit he speaketh mysteries".**

Verse four, "He that speaketh in an unknown tongue edifieth himself…" Again, he is edifying himself, not man and not the church.

In **verse five, "I would that ye all spake with tongues…"** This is the desire of the Holy Spirit, that everyone is filled, speaking in tongues. Everyone, in a worship service, could be speaking in tongues at once, and there would be no confusion, because they're speaking to God and not man. That is what happened on the Day of Pentecost. They were all speaking in tongues at the same time!

Now the Holy Spirit changes direction. He begins talking about the gifts of the Spirit operating. No longer is He talking about an individual speaking in his prayer language. In the middle portion of **verse five,** we find this statement, **"…for greater is he that prophesieth than he that speaketh with tongues…"**

He is referring to two different gifts: the gifts of **tongues and prophecy.** Is that the end of the statement? No, that is not the end of the statement! If that were the end of the statement, then you could say, "That's it…I want to prophesy, because it is better than speaking in tongues".

There are a lot of people who get hung up on **1 Corinthians 12:31 "But covet earnestly the best gifts: and yet shew I unto you a more excellent way".** They wonder how you can determine the best gifts.

Now bear in mind, the gifts are only for the Spirit-filled. **1 Corinthians 12:11 "But all these worketh that one and the selfsame Spirit, dividing to every man severally as he will".** The Holy Spirit must have yielded vessels through which He can flow, in order to use them.

I look over the church and see all kinds of needs. There are people who need to be healed of all kinds of chronic diseases and infirmities. I've often thought "if I had the **Gifts of Healing and Miracles** operating in my life, I would go to every hospital, and start on the top floor and work my way down, laying hands on everyone, until I would empty the hospital". I would go to every home where someone was sick and pray for them. There is never a failure when the gifts are operating! The Lord does not want us sick. He has made provisions for our healing. He declared to the children of Israel in **Exodus 15:26 "...for I am the Lord that healeth thee".** That expresses His desire, but it was contingent upon the children of Israel obeying His Word and keeping His commandments!

I've also thought, if I had the gift of **Faith** operating all the time, I could believe the Lord for other things that would be helpful in the ministry.

Then, there are a lot of things I wished I knew, that I don't know, that would perhaps make my ministry a lot easier. So, I thought if I just had the gifts of **Wisdom or Knowledge** operating it would help me.

All of the gifts seem important to us, but what is the best gift?

For the sake of illustration, let me explain it this way. Let's say, for example, a sanctuary is a large cabinet shop. On one wall, there are nine new saws, the very best that can be made. On the other side of the wall, is a craftsman, who is working. All of a sudden he cries out, "Hey, bring me the best saw"! I look and see the nine saws, and I know there is a question I must ask: "What are you doing"? He cries, "I need to cut a steel bolt". I look on the wall and see a coping saw. I know a coping saw will not cut a steel bolt. I see a ten-point hand saw a trim carpenter would use. I know it will not cut a steel bolt. But, I see a hacksaw on the wall. I take it to the craftsman, and he says, "That's exactly what I need to get the job done"! The problem is not, is one saw better than another. The problem is, "What does God want you to do"?

I haven't told you what the best gift is, but I have told you how you can find it. What needs to be done in the church? In the power equipment of the Holy Spirit, there is equipment for anything the Lord may call you to do.

The Lord wants **all the gifts** operating in the church! I'm afraid we are out of balance when it comes to the operation of the gifts in our churches. We often have **Tongues and Interpretation of Tongues,** but where are the other seven gifts?

1 Corinthians 14:26 states "How is it then, brethren? When ye come together, every one of you hath a psalm, hath a doctrine, hath a tongue, hath a revelation, hath an interpretation. Let all things be done unto edifying". The Lord's plan for us is to be prayed up and full of the Holy Spirit when we come to church, so the Holy Spirit can flow through us and use us in the operation of the gifts, that the church may be edified! We all are to have a part in the service!

Can you imagine what would begin happening, if people who are lame and blind or deaf or battling cancer, would come to church and the gifts of **Healing or Miracles** were operating? They would leave, healed by the power of God! Our churches could not hold the crowds. That is exactly what the Lord wants! He has given us the means whereby that can happen.

He wants us to be channels through which He can flow. All too often we are "under-hungry" for the things of the Spirit. We must yield ourselves into His hands, so He can guide us, and direct us and draw us closer to Him. He said, **"Blessed are they which do hunger and thirst after righteousness: for they shall be filled".**

I'll never forget, as a young man, attending Southwestern Pentecostal Holiness Bible School in Oklahoma City, we had gathered for chapel service, when they brought one of the students who had fallen and broken his leg, into chapel. He asked to be brought to chapel, before they took him to the hospital. You could see he was in excruciating pain as the president of the school, the dean of men, and all the teachers and professors, began praying for him. As we all prayed, the Holy Spirit spoke to my heart "Go, lay your hands on him and pray". I wrestled with the Lord and said, "But Lord, I am no one". The Holy Spirit kept speaking, "Go, lay your hands on him and pray"! I stood there until I thought my heart would jump out of my body, because it was pounding so hard. I began crying and finally said "Lord, if you want me to go and lay my hands on him and pray, I will". I walked up the isle to where they were praying for him, and reached over, and laid my hands on him and asked the Lord to heal him. Instantly, the Lord healed him! His leg was straightened as it snapped back into place! The Lord will use yielded vessels that are hungry to be used by God! The gift of **Miracles** was in operation, because I had always wanted to be used by the Lord, and I was full of the Holy Spirit. **"These signs shall follow them that believe…" Mark 16:17.**

If you're a believer and filled with the Holy Spirit, you can be used of God! Don't sit back and wait and say, "It's not for me. It's just for those in leadership", because God wants to use those who are filled with the Holy Spirit.

Several years ago, when I was pastor at Faith Tabernacle, in Oklahoma City, I was singing, "I Must Tell Jesus", in the Sunday morning service. There is a place in the song where I go up to sing a number of high notes in a row. While I was singing the high part, I suddenly felt sharp pains in my chest. It almost took my breath away, but I was able to finish the song. I was able to preach when I finished the song, but had suddenly become very weak. I stood behind the pulpit and just talked my message, instead of preaching the way I normally would. When I finished the sermon, I asked the people to come to the altars to pray. I caught my wife's attention, and asked her to come to the platform. I explained what had happened and that we would need to go home as soon as the altar service was over. We took both of our children and went immediately home instead of going out to eat as we normally did.

That afternoon I could not breath without pain and shortness of breath. Gretnia wanted to take me to the hospital, but I would not let her. She wanted to call our family members and people of the church to pray, but again, I didn't want her to. I told her we needed to be in church that evening, because we had a special guest scheduled. As the afternoon progressed, my breathing became more and more labored.

We went to the church that evening, even though I was having difficulty breathing. The choir had finished singing when Gloria Fajardo, current pastor of Cathedral of the Palms in Corpus Christi, Texas, asked my Minister of Music, present missionary to Malawi, Dean Galyen, if she could share something with the church she had felt in her prayer time that afternoon. She went to the pulpit and told the church the Lord had revealed to her that afternoon I needed healing. She then asked the church to join her in prayer to pray for me. I went to the pulpit and shared with the church what had happened that morning and that I did indeed need prayer.

She led the church in prayer and when she finished, a message in tongues and the interpretation was given. The Lord said He was there to heal if we would only believe. When the interpretation was finished, I felt warmth that began at the top of my head and coursed down through my body. When it reached my chest, suddenly the pain and shortness of breath were gone! I could breath deeply. The Lord had healed my body!! The gifts of the Spirit were operating in the church!

I asked for everyone who needed prayer for healing to come forward. I told the church the gifts of faith, miracles and healing were operating. I was amazed as almost 350 people lined up around the sanctuary. We began praying and people were slain under the power all over the church. They lay prostrate all over the front of the church, down the isles, and in between the pews. It was a sovereign move of the Holy Spirit! It all began that evening because someone relatively new in the Lord at that time, obeyed the leading of the Holy Spirit, and allowed the gifts to operate in her life.

I went to the doctor shortly after that experience, and he did an EKG and verified I had had a heart attack, but the Lord had healed me.

Paul, under the inspiration of the Holy Spirit, said in **verse five, "...for greater is he that prophesieth than he that speaketh with tongues..."** and then he goes on to say, **"...except he interpret, that the church may receive edifying".** Many people stop after the first portion of this statement. Don't ever take a little piece out of the middle of a verse and fasten a doctrine on it! That's one of the most dangerous things you can possibly do.

Paul is dealing with the **gift of tongues,** which is one of the nine gifts of the Spirit. Again, this is a different kind of speaking in tongues than we've dealt with previously. This has to do with the edifying of the church. The other had to do with our communion and fellowship with God in prayer!

You can always tell which is which. If it speaks of prayer, praise or worship, it is your prayer language, which you pour out to God and it is divine secrets between you and the Lover of your soul. But, if it is the gift, then, from the heart of God, a message by the Spirit, through the Spirit-filled believer, and the people are the goal of what is being said.

They cannot be exactly the same because they are going in opposite directions! They have different purposes! They provide different results!

When we're speaking in tongues, pouring out our heart's desire, praying in the Spirit, God is the goal. This is going from man to God! Man is edified.

When God wants to speak to the church, then He chooses one person to give a message in tongues, commanding the attention of the believers. It comes from the heart of God, going to the church, that the church may be edified.

Paul gives us the order of the usage of the gifts of **tongues and interpretation of tongues** in **1 Corinthians 14:27 "If any man speak in an unknown tongue, let it be by two, or at the most by three, and that by course: and let one interpret".** You can tell he is speaking of the gift of tongues and not our prayer language. He says there are to be no more than three messages in tongues in any one service. Any more than that is out of order. I have been in services where there have been many more than that. This occurs because of lack of knowledge and teaching.

He said in **verse 28 "But if there be no interpreter, let him keep silence in the church; and let him speak to himself, and to God".** If a person gives a message in tongues, it is their responsibility to give the interpretation, is what Paul is saying. Many times, messages are given, and you have a long awkward time before anyone gives the interpretation, if they are interpreted. Paul said in **verse 33 "For God is not the author of confusion, but of peace, as in all churches of the saints".** There is confusion if a message is not interpreted.

Paul said in **verse 29 "Let the prophets speak two or three, and let the other judge".** He is saying you can have three prophetic utterances in a service, and that is perfectly in order. When you go beyond that, you are in the flesh and not the Spirit.

All of these things happen in and through us because we have been filled with the Holy Spirit. He wants us as individuals to grow and be strengthened in the Lord. He wants the church to grow and be strengthened. So, He has made provisions for us individually, as well as for the church. **Get full of the Holy Spirit! Stay full of the Holy Spirit! "Covet earnestly the best gifts".**

There seems to be less evidence of the gifts of the Spirit than there used to be! Let me ask you, "How many of you have had, in evidence in your life, one or more of the gifts of the Spirit"? **Are you doing it now? Paul said in 2 Timothy 1:6 "...stir up the gift of God, which is in thee..." Do it now!! It is God's Word!!**

BENEFIT SIX: NO SOUND WITHOUT MEANING

1 Corinthians 14:10 "There are, it may be, so many kinds of voices in the world, and none of them is without significa- tion".

We have now gone from verse five to verse ten. **We are still on the subject of tongues!** Look at the three words, **"kinds of voices",** because they come from an ancient Greek word **"phone",** which literally means **"sounds".** The word **"signifi- cation"** in the Greek simply means **"meaning".** So, in reality, this is the way the verse would read, "There are, it may be, so many **sounds** in the world, and none of them is without **mean- ing".**

I have heard people say, "I'm not interested in all that **"gibber- ing"** that goes on in your Pentecostal churches". **The Holy Spirit does not gibber!** When He gives us an utterance, He doeth all things well! When He begins speaking through a believer, it has a meaning, whether to God in prayer or praise, or to believers in the gifts of the Spirit.

There may be some who say, "Well, I don't like the sound!" So what!? We're not talking to you...we're talking to God! And, whatever sound the Holy Spirit gives you to speak with your tongue, has a meaning to God. As far as the words, the annunci- ation, the combination of words, why should you have to like it? We're speaking to God!

One of our Assembly of God pastors shared his experience of receiving the Baptism of the Holy Spirit. He said when he first received the Baptism, it bothered him that every word he spoke ended in an open vowel sound. He could not understand why his prayer language sounded that way, until he had a missionary from Tanzania, for a service. The missionary asked if he would like to see the Bible, which had been translated into the Tanzanian language. To his amazement, every word ended in an open vowel sound! When the missionary spoke the name of Paul, it sounded like "Paulee".

Then the missionary asked, "How do you like this sound? E,C,C,C,C". It doesn't make any sense to us, but to the Tanzanians, it meant a young lady was walking down the jungle trail in the cool of the evening!

I have been in services when a short message in tongues would be given, followed by a longer interpretation. I've then heard someone say, "Well, whoever gave the interpretation sure missed it, because the interpretation was longer than the message". It's ridiculous to try and bring God down to our level, with our little finite minds! We try to make Him no bigger than what we can comprehend.

You hear someone give a message in tongues and there are a number of strange sounds, coming together, that sound to you exactly alike and you say, "Well, I don't like that, there should be more of a variety, they should do that a little better". But, in the midst of it, God Almighty is listening and He knows the meaning! You know, since it is God-ward, or to be interpreted, we don't have to pigeonhole everything, and say, "I like it this way, or I don't like it that way". You not only waste your time, but you hurt the feelings of the Holy Spirit!

I heard one of our preachers tell the story of a lady whose husband moved his family up into the Cascade Mountains. They were so far back they could not get out to go to church. After a period of time she grew cold and backslid.

After twenty years they moved back into town. The first Sunday night back in town she went to the Assembly of God church where she gave her heart back to the Lord. Then she began seeking for the Baptism of the Holy Spirit. When she went through to the Baptism, she made just one sound, over and over again.

The pastors had been missionaries to Tanzania before they became pastors of the church, and when the woman began making the one sound, the pastor's wife called her husband and said "We have not heard that sound since we left Tanzania". She said that was a sound so difficult to make because of the way our Western tongue works, that she and her husband had never been able to speak it well. Yet, this woman was saying it with absolute perfection.

And, the word she was using, was a word the natives used when they saw someone they had not seen for a while, whom they loved and honored, and they would bend over at the waist and extend their hands toward that person, speaking the sound over and over again, as they backed down the trail that led to their hut.

After twenty years, the Holy Spirit reached over into a Tanzanian village, and brings, not a multiplicity of sounds, but one sound, over and over, to welcome Him back into her heart. **"There's not a sound in the world without meaning"! Oh, we need a love for what the Holy Spirit does!**

In one of our camp meetings, during a prayer meeting one day, there was an explosion of tongues by an individual. It was just one word said over and over.

Some people, even in prayer meetings, are not always in tune with what the Holy Spirit wants. It's not enough to just kneel and pray. We need to yield ourselves to the Holy Spirit.

The sound that was being made was so irritating to some of the people, they asked some of the pastors to go over and quieten the person down. They said he was interrupting the prayer meeting.

About that time, coming down the isle, was a missionary from Africa. As he and his friend were walking, he stopped and said "What about that? I've not heard that sound in years, but that's the sound our natives made when their king was walking in their midst"! **There was a King walking there all the time!!** And yet, there were some who didn't want that person to express what the Holy Spirit gave him to express. The sound had not made any sense to them. But, the person was not speaking to them, he was speaking to God! Whatever the Holy Spirit gives us to speak, has a meaning to God.

When I was pastor of Faith Tabernacle in Oklahoma City, I had a couple, who each time I gave an invitation for those who wanted to receive the Baptism, would come forward. Every time I prayed for them, they would begin speaking in tongues. I would then ask, "Well, what has the Lord done for you tonight"?

I have always wanted people to tell me if they have received the Baptism. I don't tell them they have received. I think we make a big mistake when we tell someone they have received the Holy Spirit! They need to know for themselves what the Lord has done for them.

It is not a matter of getting people to say, "Peter Piper picked a peck of pickled peppers", as fast as they can and then tell them, they have received the Baptism when their tongue gets tangled. **The Holy Spirit does not need our help!**

One night I asked the couple what they were expecting to happen when they were filled? They told me when they were young, they had a couple that was friends, and they were with them when they received the Holy Spirit. The couple told them when they received the Holy Spirit they would sound just like they sounded and they had never sounded like the other couple.

As a result, they never accepted the Baptism. You have to accept what the Spirit gives you and use it before He gives you more! I prayed and prayed with them but they never accepted the Baptism while we were there.

The devil is going to do anything he can to keep you from receiving the Holy Spirit. He will cause you to doubt what you have received. He will make you think it is you speaking instead of the Holy Spirit. He will make you think you are making something up. He will make you think you are mocking the Holy Spirit. But, how can you mock the Holy Spirit? **You don't know what sound He may give you to speak to God!**

As you yield to the Holy Spirit, the more you use your prayer language, the clearer it will become. It's just like a baby when it is born. The baby does not come out of it's mother's womb speaking. It does not look up and say, "Hi, mom". That baby does not talk. It lies in its crib for months, listening to its mom and dad, bending over, saying, "Say, mom-ma, dad-da". Then finally, the baby makes a sound that sounds like "mom-ma or dad-da", and that mom and dad gets so excited because the baby is talking. Is it speaking clear words? No. It's speaking the sounds it has been hearing. The more the baby speaks the sounds, the clearer the sounds become. The baby will continue to speak more and more "sounds" as he or she hears them. The baby learns to speak by hearing the different words spoken to him or her and then, it will speak those words.

Do not be afraid to speak whatever the Holy Spirit gives you to speak. The sounds you are making, God understands! **"There's not a sound in the world without a meaning", when it is spoken to God!**

In July of 2000, I was invited to preach the General Council of the Assemblies of God in Malawi, Africa. The first night my wife and I were sitting in the congregation, enjoying the anointed music, when all of a sudden, directly behind us, a lady broke out in a high-pitched voice, making an unusual sound. The tongue, moving rapidly, made the sound, as though she was blowing with her tongue. All over the congregation, many others, doing the same thing, repeated the sound. To Gretnia and me, it did not make any sense, but to them, they were worshipping their God with a sound of praise. **"There's not a sound in the world without meaning"**!

The Holy Spirit gives us a **sound from heaven. Acts 2:2 "And suddenly there came a sound from heaven as of a rushing mighty wind, and it filled all the house where they were sitting".** He gives us the sound, but we must make the sound.

On the day of Pentecost, the Holy Spirit did not speak one word. **Acts 2:4 "And <u>they were all filled</u> with the Holy Ghost, and <u>began to speak with other tongues,</u> as the Spirit gave them utterance".** They were speaking, not the Holy Spirit!

It's like two people speaking at the same time. The Spirit gives the utterance, but we must do the speaking. The Holy Spirit has to use our tongue, lips, voice, mind and body. He must have a channel through which He can flow.

The sound, which came from heaven, was as of a rushing mighty wind! The word **"sound",** in the Greek is **"echos".** The word "**wind",** in the Greek is **"pnoe".** It literally meant there was a loud noise, **"an echo",** which came from heaven of the **"breath of God". God was breathing on the upper room!** We need that sound repeated often in all our churches!

The word **"rushing",** in the Greek is **"enegko",** which means, **"to carry".** The word **"mighty",** in the Greek is **"biaios",** which means **"violent".** That simply meant the **"loud noise of the breath of God was being carried violently, like a tornado, from heaven".** When the breath of God hit the upper room, all were filled with the Holy Spirit and began speaking in other tongues as the Spirit gave them utterance. It was like a tornado had struck, for they went forth and began turning the world upside down! Cloven tongues like as of a fire, like lightning flashes, sat upon each one of them. They were infused with power from on high!

Oh, do it again Lord!! We need an infusion of power as well, to accomplish what the Lord wants and expects, in our churches today!!

BENEFIT SEVEN: PRAYING AND SINGING WITH THE SPIRIT

1 Corinthians 14:15 "What is it then? I will pray with the spirit, and I will pray with the understanding also: I will sing with the spirit, and I will sing with the understanding also".

Paul is saying we can pray in tongues, or by the Spirit, and we can pray with the interpretation of our prayers as well. We can sing in tongues and sing with the interpretation of tongues also. What a tremendous blessing and benefit is ours, all because we have been filled with the Holy Spirit! This is part of a "wholly" overflow. We get so full we can't contain all the blessings.

There are some people that look at Pentecostal believers and think when we speak in tongues that it just can't quite be right. They think we're about half a bubble off level because they can't understand what's happening in our lives.

There's something a little psychological here that's interesting to look at. If you approach a subject from the wrong direction, you're going to reach the wrong conclusion. If you study the Bible to see what is **wrong** with speaking in other tongues, then the entire matter will be warped before you reach the conclusion.

If you approach the matter of speaking in other tongues, as though there is something wrong with it, then the devil will do one of two things: Either he will help you find something that you think is right, or he will bend the Word before it ever reaches your heart and you will not see it clearly as God has declared in His Word.

This matter of speaking in other tongues is absolutely beautiful. I've said it before, but it bears repeating. Speaking in tongues were never meant to be argumentative or controversial. The Baptism of the Holy Spirit was meant to be spoken; it was meant to be experienced.

It's wonderful that those who have followed our Lord, including Jesus' own mother, received the Baptism of the Holy Spirit and spoke in other tongues as the Spirit gave utterance. If it were good enough for them, it's good enough for us!

The Lord has never changed! He's the same yesterday, today and forever!

Mary was a tongue-talking mother! Praise God!! Every child, in all our churches, need a mother and dad who are tongue-talking moms and dads. If you have robbed your children of that marvelous experience, you have done an injustice and disservice to them. You may have provided everything they need materially, but the material things are not going to qualify them for heaven. Material things will not help you be a better spiritual leader. Getting full of the Holy Spirit and staying full will help you in every way!

What will help our children get to heaven is the spiritual leadership provided by Spirit-filled moms and dads. Our kids need to see our dedication, our consecration and how we learn to yield to the Holy Spirit. Our kids are often as confused as a termite in a yo-yo. When it comes to the things of the Spirit, what they see and hear in their homes versus what they see and hear at church are two different things.

Parents can often be spiritual at home, but the drive to the church becomes an adventure, as parents lash out and use sharply worded statements at each other, not indicative of a person who is supposed to be filled with the Spirit. Then, when they arrive at church, presto, they have become spiritual leaders.

May we get so full of the Holy Spirit, that we: pray in the Spirit, sing in the Spirit, walk in the Spirit, let the Spirit flow through us, be sensitive to the Spirit, be led by the Spirit, in every area of our lives.

A few years ago we would never have thought the horrible monster of divorce would enter the church the way it has. I believe one simple reason that divorce has become prevalent in the church, is because husbands and wives have stopped praying and seeking God. No longer do they read and hide the Word in their hearts. No longer are people full of the Holy Spirit. They have gotten into the flesh, and begun doing what is right in their own sight.

In the many years I have spent as a pastor, I cannot tell you how many couples I have counseled. It was always sad when I would give them what I felt the Word of God would say about something, and have them say "Pastor, we know what God says in His Word, but we also know God is a forgiving God and He will forgive us, because divorce is not an unpardonable sin". Then, they would get up and walk out, oblivious to the consequences of what would happen to their children or their home. Doing it all to satisfy the flesh.

You will never find anyone who is full of the Holy Spirit wanting a divorce! It just doesn't equate! The fruits of the Spirit are found in **Galatians 5:22,23 "But the fruit of the Spirit is love, joy, peace, longsuffering, gentleness, goodness, faith, Meekness, temperance: against such there is no law".** When you get full of the Holy Spirit these fruits will be evident. You will be longsuffering in your marriage. Your marriage will be filled with love. You will experience peace. You will be gentle. You will be happy. You will have faith that things can be worked out. You will not look for ways or reasons or excuses to get a divorce!

Again, something I mentioned earlier, if you approach a subject from the wrong direction, you would get a wrong conclusion. The devil has come into our churches and brought such deception, that we have believed his lies.

I promise you, if you get full of the Holy Spirit, **there is not a problem in your home with your children or your companion,** but what can be totally and completely resolved! The Blessed Holy Spirit will put every thing back together. This is one reason the Lord wants us all filled with the Holy Spirit!

Do you realize that a person who was filled with the Holy Spirit and spoke in tongues wrote every book in the New Testament? Not one word but what fell from the pen of a tongues-talking person! The Lord wants all of us to be filled so He can use us!

Paul said in **1 Corinthians 14:14 "For if I pray in an unknown tongue, <u>my spirit prayeth,</u> but my understanding is unfruitful".**

First, we do not receive the Baptism of the Holy Spirit as a **physical experience!** It is not our body that gets the Baptism.

When Adam and Eve sinned in the Garden of Eden, there was a double curse that fell upon mankind. **First, death to the spirit that could commune with God!** When God came into the garden He could not find them. **Genesis 3:9 "And the Lord God called unto Adam, and said unto him, where art thou"?** Why couldn't He find them? Spiritual death had taken place, and God could not find them because that spirit had been broken. No longer were they living in innocence.

Then, **there was sickness, disease and death that came to the human body!** When it comes to the matter of the body, it is not as strong as it should be. Have you ever noticed, you get down to pray, and your knees begin aching? You raise your hands, and unless you are really in the Spirit, they feel as though they weigh a ton. You bow your head, and it isn't long until you get a crick in your neck. You start to kneel down, and your back starts creaking and you get a catch in your get-a-long! Your body is showing the evidence of what happened in the Garden of Eden.

Aren't you glad you don't get the baptism on our physical bodies?

Secondly, we can be happy **we don't get the baptism on our brain!** It is not a mental experience. We do not have the brain today that Adam had. Think about it…God parades all the animals before Adam and he had such mental capacity, that he named every one! Why name them if you can't remember their names? He remembered them all!

Have you ever gone blank trying to remember the names of your children? You will start to call one of them, but wind up calling all the rest of their names before you get to the one you wanted.

What ever you do, don't forget the name of your companion when you start telling them you love them!

I'm glad we don't get the baptism on our brains. Some would have a tremendous experience and some would be left out in the cold! God didn't do it that way, because the brain is still prone to the weaknesses of the original sin.
I hope you are ready to put on your shouting clothes! I pray you're ready to get happy!

There is a third part of us! We are a triune being! We are not just body and soul; we have a spirit as well. **The spirit of man is the part, which knows.** David said in **Psalms 51:10 "Create in me a clean heart, O God; and renew a right spirit within**

me". What He put in you and me, the moment we were born again, is not prone to the original curse of the garden of Eden, because **we are a new creature in Christ Jesus!!** Old things are passed away and all things have become new again! When we come to know Jesus as Lord and Savior, in that moment, the curse of sin in the Garden of Eden is destroyed. The part of us that receives the Holy Spirit is the renewed spirit that has been given to us by the Lord Himself.

This new spirit is the part of me that God put here to commune with Him! **John 4:24 "God is a Spirit: and they that worship him must worship him <u>in spirit</u> and in truth".**

There are those who try to worship Him with their bodies! I have read the stories, as well as seen pictures of a man crawling five miles to the top of a hill, with cactus weighed down with stones, tied to his back, to show his God how much he loved him. It is sad to see those who know no better!

What a difference when you become Pentecostal!

There are those who operate only on how they feel! The soul of man is the part, which feels. They have to feel good before they can worship. The only case recorded in Scripture where a man depended upon feeling, was deceived. Jacob and Rebekah deceived Isaac when she put the skins of the kids, of the goats, upon the hands and neck of Jacob. Isaac felt of Jacob and thought Jacob was Esau. If you depend upon the flesh, then you will miss the true blessing of worshipping the Lord.

There is a third part of us that was created to commune directly with the Lord! We are to speak to the Lord out of our hearts! Matthew 12:34 "...for out of the abundance of the heart the mouth speaketh".

What comes out of your mouth? Is it dirty jokes? Is it filthy languages? Do you stand around at work and laugh when other people tell their off-colored stories? Every day you go without praying in the Spirit, you're allowing the devil to tear you down more and more. As your spirit gets weaker and weaker, the flesh will get stronger and stronger, until the flesh takes control, and the spirit is put under subjection to the flesh, instead of the flesh being subject to the spirit.

Paul spoke about this in **Romans 7:18-23 "For I know that in me (that is, in my flesh,) dwelleth no good thing: for to will is present with me; but how to perform that which is good I find not. For the good that I would I do not: but the evil which I would not, that I do. Now if I do that I would not, it is no more I that do it, but sin that dwelleth in me. I find then a law, that, when I would do good, evil is present with me. For I delight in the law of God after the inward man: But I see another law in my members, warring against the law of my mind, and bringing me into captivity to the law of sin which is in my members".** There is that constant battle being waged within us. The key to us living a victorious life is getting full of the Holy Spirit, and staying full.

What nationality is the Holy Spirit, who comes to dwell within us? **He is not of this world! He's from another world!**

The Holy Spirit is the speaking member of the Godhead! When He comes in and fills us, we begin speaking what He gives us to speak. Our hearts are full of the blessings of the Lord. We will pray with the Spirit, we will sing with the Spirit, because that is what is in our heart.

The Holy Spirit is what causes Jesus to become the most important person in our lives!

The Holy Spirit is the One Who told us we are sinners!

The Holy Spirit is the One Who tells us Jesus is enough! He'll supply all our needs; take care of all our sicknesses and diseases, and all our hurts!

The carnal man cannot discern the things of the Spirit. **1 Corinthians 3:14 "But the natural man receiveth not the things of the Spirit of God: for they are foolishness unto him; neither can he know them, because they are spiritually discerned".** They cannot understand all this business about the Holy Spirit. They think we're fanatics, and none of this business of speaking in tongues is necessary.

But then, the blessed Holy Spirit begins witnessing to our hearts that we are a child of the King, an heir of God, a joint heir with Jesus Christ. And here is the Holy Spirit, that non-national Holy Spirit, Who comes from another world, that speaking part of the Godhead, and He comes in and fills us and wants to communicate with the Father and Son, Who are still in heaven.

The Holy Spirit has come to dwell on earth and abide with us forever. **John 14:16 "And I will pray the Father, and he shall give you another Comforter, that he may abide with you for ever".** When we are filled with the Holy Spirit, speaking in other tongues, we are communicating with the Father. We are not communicating with our heads or our bodies, but by our spirits. The speaking part of the Godhead moves into this non-national speaking part of me and communicates with the Father.

Wouldn't that be strange, with that combination, that there would be no speaking? If He comes in and fills me, and I never yield myself to Him, so He can speak through me to the Father, then I have missed the blessing He intended me to receive.

It takes no more faith to receive the Baptism than it does to be saved! Both experiences are received by faith. **Ephesians 2:8 "For by grace are ye saved through faith; and that not of yourselves: it is the gift of God".** Luke 11:13 **"If ye then, being evil, know how to give good gifts unto your children, how much more shall your heavenly Father give the Holy Spirit to them that ask him"?**

We don't have to take a correspondent course on how to speak in other tongues! Don't waste your time in buying a book! You don't try and teach children in Sunday School how to speak in tongues as I have seen some try and do. I know of one church where they literally tried to teach the children different sounds to make, and then told them they had received the Baptism. Things like that concern me. **The Holy Spirit doesn't need our help!**

I had one lady in our revivals that tried to shake the Holy Spirit into you. She would get you on each side of your mouth with her hand and shake your head from side to side. She loved the Lord and was sincere, but she was trying to help the Holy Spirit.

We don't have to teach people. The Holy Spirit gives the utterance! He's the speaking member of the Godhead. **Acts 2:4 "And they were all filled with the Holy Ghost, and began to speak with other tongues, as the Spirit gave them utterance". "…They…began to speak with other tongues…"**

You have to learn to speak your own native language! When you have learned it, you have learned it with your brain. You have to develop and mature and learn to speak your language.

But, when it comes to being filled with the Holy Spirit, you speak as the Spirit gives you the words. When a person begins speaking in other tongues, it becomes their prayer language, given them by the Holy Spirit.

1 Corinthians 14:14 "For if I pray in an unknown tongue, my spirit prayeth…" That's why it's so good to speak in tongues! It feels good to feel good! **"…But my understanding is unfruitful".** This is not a mental operation!

You don't turn it on and off anytime you want to with your mind! The Holy Spirit directs what is happening. We must be obedient to the Holy Spirit!

Now notice in **verse 15 "…I will pray with the spirit…"** What does that mean? **Praying in other tongues! And, "…I will pray with the understanding also…"**

There is a teaching in some charismatic circles that I feel is totally contrary to Scripture. They say, "I can speak in tongues any time I want to". You speak, **"as the Spirit gives the utterance".** A person can receive the Baptism, speak in other tongues, then backslide and continue to speak the sound or utterance they had received. I have witnessed that in lives of people.

But, it's not the Holy Spirit that is speaking, because the Holy Spirit will not dwell in an unclean temple. You don't turn it on and off any time you want to without the Spirit quickening you!

We are to be led **by the Spirit** instead of leading the Spirit! We get the cart before the horse. **"My spirit prayeth…"** the Spirit **has given it to me!** So, what does that mean? It means I will pray with other tongues and with my understanding also.

One should never get so spiritual that you no longer pray in your own language! There must be a holy balance. Marvelous is the privilege of speaking in other tongues in our prayer to God, but it does not supersede everything else. It is a wonderful and supernatural additive to an already marvelous prayer life.

Let the Holy Spirit move and have His way. Pray in your own language so you can have understanding, but pray also in the Spirit. The Holy Spirit has given us a balance!

I have watched too many people down through the years, which have come into Pentecost, wanting to receive all the Lord had for them, and wound up missing the boat completely. They wanted to be spiritual, and wound up being super-spiritual. They claimed they spoke in tongues continually. **That's a danger!**

I remember one lady who began attending one of the churches we pastored in Oklahoma City. She and her husband came from another denomination, which did not believe in speaking in tongues. She received the Baptism and became what I call a super-spiritual Christian.

She came by the church one day to talk to my wife and me, and informed us the Lord told her to divorce her husband. We told her the Lord had done no such thing, that He does not go contrary to His Word. That happens when you get out of balance in the things of the Spirit. There was no way of convincing her she was wrong. God had told her to divorce her husband and who were we to say He hadn't.

Get full of the Holy Spirit, be led by the Spirit, and hide yourself away in the Word so you know what the Word has to say. The devil can see hungry hearts, and knows you want everything the Lord has for you. Unless you stay grounded in the Word and what the Spirit has to say to you, you can get out of balance and be deceived.

1 Corinthians 14:15 "…I will sing with the spirit, and I will sing with the understanding also". Have you ever sung in the Spirit?

The mood of a **nation** can be determined by its music!
The mood of a **church** can be determined by its music!
The mood of a **person** can be determined by his music!
If that is the case, then we're in trouble! Many of our churches are having trouble because of the music. There is a simple key to unlocking the door to perfect harmony. **Get full of the Holy Spirit and be led by the Spirit! Pray in the Spirit, sing in the Spirit, be sensitive to the Holy Spirit and He will give the music He wants!**

There is a tremendous blessing to singing in the Spirit. It becomes a heavenly act. As we yield to the Spirit, the Spirit flows through us, giving us a song in our hearts. **Psalms 40:3**

"And he hath put a new song in my mouth, even praise unto our God: many shall see it, and fear, and shall trust in the Lord". Many times I have sung in tongues. On two different occasions, I have been in services where people would understand what I was singing, as I sang in the Cherokee Indian language.

I have been where someone would sing a message in tongues and, then, sing the interpretation. The church was blessed and edified. The gifts of the Spirit were operating and the Lord was speaking to His people. This is His plan for all our churches.

We do not see as much of this in our churches as the Lord wants. He wants to come and move among us. He wants us to experience times of refreshing and blessing. He wants all the gifts of the Spirit operating. **Pray in the Spirit, sing in the Spirit. Be a channel through which the Spirit of the Lord can move!**

BENEFIT EIGHT: THIS IS THE REST

1 Corinthians 14:21 "In the law it is written, With men of other tongues and other lips will I speak unto this people; and yet for all that will they not hear me, saith the Lord".

You know immediately when you read this, that this is a quotation from Old Testament writings; writings that were written 700 years before Christ. Paul was being moved upon by the Holy Spirit to reach back into the Old Testament and bring out something on the subject of speaking in other tongues.

Let's go back to **Isaiah 28** and look at **verses 11 and 12** and see to what Paul was referring. **"For with stammering lips and another tongue will he speak to this people. To whom he said, This is the rest wherewith ye may cause the weary to rest; and this is the refreshing: yet they would not hear".**

When you read these words in the Old Testament, it's enough to make you want to shout! This is coming directly from heaven! The Lord is saying, **"For with stammering lips and another tongue will he speak to his people". This is speaking in tongues!**

There are a lot of people who deeply love the Word of God who are not the least bit interested in speaking in other tongues. There comes a place where they just cut it off and say, "I'm not interested in that".

I want to show you in this portion of Scripture what Isaiah the prophet had to say about people who are not interested in speaking in other tongues.

Let's go back to **verse 9, "Whom shall he teach knowledge? And whom shall he make to understand doctrine? Them that are weaned from the milk, and drawn from the breasts".** That means, not for the immature, not for babies.

Paul said in **1 Corinthians 3:1,2 "And I, brethren, could not speak unto you as unto spiritual, but as unto carnal, even as unto babes in Christ. I have fed you with milk, and not with meat: for hitherto ye were not able to bear it, neither yet now are ye able".** Why did he continue to give them milk? Because they were not spiritually mature.

One of the most discouraging things you run into as a pastor is that you want to give your people meat, but you can't, because you have to keep giving them milk. You have to take the baby bottle, part the whiskers and the mustache, to get the bottle in, and keep giving them milk instead of giving them meat. They may look mature, but have never grown up. They are still babies. This is true in the lives of too many people.

Isaiah 28: 10: "For precept must be upon precept, precept upon precept; line upon line, line upon line; here a little, and

there a little". The ones of whom he is speaking, the ones who will come to maturity, are those who want, literally, the Word of God! <u>You</u> **cannot set any doctrine on anything other than the Word of God!**

If a person only goes so far, they come into great danger. And, for the person who loves God's Word, **"...precept upon precept, line upon line..."** suddenly they come to this in God's Word. **Verses 11 & 12 "For with stammering lips and another tongue will he speak to this people. To whom he said, This is the rest wherewith ye may cause the weary to rest; and this is the refreshing..."**

When a person who loves the Word, suddenly sees tongues in the Bible, a decision must immediately be made! Will I receive God's Word on that or will I not?

Look at the latter part of **verse 12 "...yet they <u>would not hear</u>".**

Verse 13: "But the word of the Lord was unto them...(<u>These are the ones who wouldn't hear about tongues</u>)...precept upon precept, precept upon precept; line upon line, line upon line; here a little, and there a little".

And now, immediately, you find what happens to them who face the doctrine, the teaching, if you will, of the Upper Room, and then turn their back upon it! **"...That they might go, and fall backward, and be broken, and snared, and taken".** In other words, losing the ground they had gained as they were studying the Word, **"...precept upon precept, line upon line..."** and then they become broken and snared. The devil uses this to take many people away from what God has for them, and the Word says they are taken, falling back, ensnared.

Yes, they loved the Word **until it came to the subject of tongues.** Then they said, "I'm not willing to listen to that"!

God said they would not, He didn't say they could not. There is a world of difference in **not being able to hear and not being willing to hear!** He said those who faced the teaching of the Upper Room and have turned their backs upon it experienced this, **"...that they might go, and fall backward, and be broken, and snared, and taken".**

We should not be too hard on people at this point. Many have turned their backs on Pentecost because it has not been made clear to them. They have seen things in Pentecost that bothered them. I have seen things that bothered me! You sometime feel that every old alley cat in the country has been thrown into Pentecost! **Many of the things that have turned people away from Pentecost are not Pentecost!** It is just something the devil has thrown in, and many times what the devil has thrown in is so vocal and so visible, that the ones who are **"under- hungry"** for Pentecost, see the scarecrows and are scared away from the very thing with which they need to be filled!

2 Timothy 2:26 "And that they may recover themselves out of the snare of the devil, who are taken captive by him at his will". The devil has laid a snare for many in the church world. Many denominations have denounced speaking in tongues, saying it is of the devil, or it is not necessary, or it is not relevant in today's world. They say, "I just love the Word of God", but, when it comes to the subject of tongues, they do not receive it and fall back, caught in the snare of the devil.

A number of years ago, when I was pastor in El Reno, Oklahoma, I had a good friend who was pastor of a church, which did not believe in speaking in tongues. He received the Baptism as well as several in his church. They were excited about their wonderful new experience and wanted to learn every thing they could. Their church did not have Sunday evening services, but began having prayer meetings in different church member's homes.

My wife and I, along with several other members of our church, were invited to one of their prayer meetings after our Sunday evening service. When we arrived at the home we were invited into the den, where a service was already in progress.

A pastor from an independent Pentecostal church in town had heard what was happening, and called and offered to help my friend understand Pentecostal worship. He and his wife were conducting the service when we arrived. His wife had one of the new converts seated in a chair in the middle of a circle. All of a sudden, she began crying, "Oh, can you see it, can you see it"? I looked as hard as I could to see about what she was talking. I could see nothing! Then she cried, "Oh, can you see the cross of blood in her forehead"? I had quite a time later trying to explain to my friend, if you can't find it in the Word of God, don't accept it.

There are a lot of weird things that go on in Pentecostal circles. They're scarecrows and alley cats the devil throws in to discourage hungry hearts.

Then the devil throws in some things that appeal to the flesh. Many people have gotten excited about gold dust. It appears in the hair of people. They shake their heads and the dust appears. I tell people, "Give me chapter and verse". Paul said in **2 Corinthians 13:1 "...In the mouth of two or three witnesses shall every word be established".**

It's no wonder some people think Pentecostals are about a half-bubble off level! It is up to us to show the world what Pentecost is really like! They need to see the power and sense the anointing of the Holy Spirit in our lives. We must walk the walk, talk the talk and live the life in lifting up the Lord. He said in **John 12:32 "And I, if I be lifted up from the earth, will draw all men unto me".**

If we live the life that exemplifies the Spirit of Almighty God flowing in our lives, they will see people who are filled with love and compassion and have an anointing on their lives, who are not afraid to testify and witness in an endeavor to lead people to Jesus. They will look at us and say, "That's what I want! I want Pentecost!! I want the power of the Holy Spirit! I want the 'real'"!

You see people who love the Word of God, who never enter into Pentecost, because they have said "no" at the moment God wanted them to say "yes". Let's pray we become more sensitive to the Holy Spirit to help them in their understanding.

Verse 11 stated, "For with stammering lips and another tongue will he speak to this people".
Verse 12 "To whom he said, This is the <u>rest</u>..."

The word **"rest"** occurs twice in this verse and I want to explain them both to you.

The first time the word **"rest"** is used, means: **"the oneness of matrimony"**. This is the **"rest"**; this is **"the oneness of matrimony"**. If you are not happily married, this may be hard to understand.

There was a time when the Lord "wooed" us as a bridegroom would "woo" his bride. The moment we said yes to Him, we became as one! Our heart beat as His heart beat. We became: **"...heirs of God, joint heirs with Jesus Christ".** We share His love for the lost. **2 Peter 3:9 "...not willing that any should perish, but that all should come to repentance".**
Then in the Upper Room, Jesus, taking us in His hands of love, those nail-printed, but power-filled, baptizing hands, immersed us in the Holy Spirit! Bringing us up from that holy experience, we then had the privilege of expressing ourselves to the lover of our souls by the power of the Holy Spirit!

That **"oneness"** with the lover of our soul is not in the fullest sense made complete, until we have this experience Paul is writing of in **1 Corinthians 14:21 "In the law it is written, With men of other tongues and other lips will I speak unto this**

people; and yet for all that will they not hear me, saith the Lord".

I want to show you where this word **"rest"** occurs in **Ruth 3:1-2.** Ruth's mother-in-law, Naomi, thinks it's time to have a heart to heart, motherly talk with Ruth. Naomi takes her aside and says**, "...My daughter, shall I not seek "rest" for thee, that it may be well with thee"? And now is not Boaz of our kindred..."** Then Naomi goes on to tell Ruth what a wonderful husband Boaz would make!

There comes a day when the Holy Spirit comes to us and says "Shall I not seek **"rest" (oneness of matrimony),** for thee, that it may be well with thee"? And now, is not Jesus the lover of our souls?

And, when we begin speaking in other tongues, the wonder, the beauty, the glow and the glory of the one to whom you have said yes, suddenly dawns upon us. **"This is the rest! This is the oneness of matrimony. This is that relationship we can never experience until we are baptized in the Holy Spirit, speaking in other tongues as the Spirit gives utterance!"**

This is one of the most glorious experiences, besides salvation, we can have on the face of the earth! I wish everyone could have this marvelous experience of the **"rest"**.

Verse 12 "...This is the "oneness of matrimony" wherewith ye may cause the weary to <u>rest</u>..." This is the second time the word **"rest"** is used in this verse. This time it's an entirely different word in the Hebrew. **"Rest"** here means: **"to abide in comfort".**

Jesus said in **John 14:16 "And I will pray the Father, and he shall give you another Comforter, that he may abide with you for ever".** When we receive the Baptism of the Holy Spirit, we do not lose the comfort of the Lord! We still have Him as that present help in time of need; the One Who sticks closer than a brother; the One Who said He would never leave us or forsake us! **We have the dual comfort of the Lord and the Holy Spirit!**

Every time we speak in tongues, it's a confirmation that the Holy Spirit is still in us as our Comforter. We know the Lord is still with us because the Holy Spirit will not dwell in an unclean temple.

The word "abide" has included in its meaning something that is permanent, something that is solid, that's staying right there.

Those who want the **"rest"** of the Holy Spirit must keep it up-to-date to maintain the abiding aspect of that holy **"rest"**. They shall **"abide in comfort"**.

For some in our churches, it seems the bond of holy matrimony with our Lord, has become a worn-out experience. This can happen in any of our marriage relationships if we don't communicate with each other. How long can a marriage last if you never express to each other your love? You will lose the excitement in your marriage. It will be dull and become an endurance test.

A lot of people do the same thing with the Lord and the Holy Spirit. They go on and on with their lives without communicating with Them. They never share how much they love Them. Oh, they want all the benefits of serving the Lord. They want Him to supply all their needs, answer all their prayers, grant all their petitions and fulfill the desires of their hearts.

They wonder why they have lost the anointing and why the Lord isn't answering their prayers? They're not abiding in comfort; they're not experiencing the rest, because they have not kept their experience up to date.

I married my wife, Gretnia, when she was sixteen. I was the ripe old age of nineteen. We really felt mature in those days. I loved her then and still tell her every day I love her. I love her more today than I did when we married. She's not only my wife; she's my best friend as well. I do not get tired of being with her. She is still my bride, and we're still on our honeymoon after more than forty-six years. Do you know why we're still together? Because it is something at which we both work! I still have the same thrill every time I look into her eyes, and say, "I love you". The "do-daddies" still run up and down my spine. That has never stopped!

The same thing is true in our relationship with the Lord. If we work hard in that relationship with the Lord, and we work as hard in our relationship with the Holy Spirit, there is no telling what our potential would be. It is up to us to keep our experiences current and up-to-date.

Every time we come together to worship Him, we should lift our hands and say, "Jesus, I love you with all my heart"! We should worship and praise Him until the Holy Spirit begins flowing, and we begin praising Him in our heavenly language.

"This is the rest, (the oneness of matrimony), wherewith the weary are made to rest, (to abide in comfort)".

Get full of the Holy Spirit, stay full, speaking in other tongues as the Spirit gives utterance.

STUDY QUESTIONS FOR BENEFIT ONE: SPEAKING TO GOD

In I Corinthians 14 (the most misunderstood chapter in the Bible) Paul deals with two ways to speak in other tonques. Explain the two.

Give a scriptual response to those who contend that speaking in unknown tongues is of the devil and not to be followed.

What are the primary purposes for God giving us the Baptism in the Holy Spirit?

Briefly explain why I Corintihians 14 is commonly called the "tongues chapter?"

The word "cloven" in the Greak means:

In I Corinthians 14:2, who is the speaker speaking to when he or she is uttering an unknown tongue?

STUDY QUESTIONS FOR BENEFIT TWO: HE SPEAKETH MYSTERIES

Who is the prince of the power of the air? In what scripture is the answer located.

What is the Greek word for "mysteries" and what does it mean.

In I Corinthians 14:2, the scripture states that when one speaks in an unknown tongue "he speaketh mysteries." What then is the purpose of speaking in tongues?

Is it possible for Satan to know what is being said when a person speaks in an unknown tongue? Explain and defend your answer.

Ephesians 2:2 tells us that Satan is..."the prince of the power of the air." Of the first, second, and third heaven, from which one is Satan totally restricted?

In Isaiah 14:12-14, in your own words, describe Lucifer's view of himself and his role in frustrating the Christian's petitions being answered.

What is meant by the statement "many times we feel that the Lord does not really care for our needs." <u>That is a lie from the pit of hell</u>!!!

How does the Lord give us the means to get our prayers answered <u>without the devil knowing</u> what our petitions are?

What is meant by the statement "The Holy Spirit comes in and begins to formulate through us, in our prayer language, the petitions going directly to the throne of God."

How do we know that the devil is not undertanding our petitions when we speak to God in tongues?

What is meant by the statement, "He [Holy Spirit] is speaking through us, directly to the Father, secret things that the devil cannot understand, because it is communication between members of the Godhead!"

List five reasons why a Christian does not receive the Baptism in the Holy Spirit. By each answer state whether the reason should be sufficient enough to delay the believer's infilling with the Holy Spirit.

STUDY QUESTIONS FOR BENEFIT THREE - HE EDIFIETH HIMSELF

List six real benefits to a Christian when he or she receives the Baptism in the Holy Spirit.

Explain what is meant by the phrase "paying tithes." (Malachi 3:8)

Why is falling in love with Jesus key to being liberal in paying your tithes and offerings. (Mark 12:30)

Name two major meanings of the Greek word "oikodomeo". (I. Corinthians 14:4) Explain both.

What is meant by the saying "my body is the temple of the Holy Spirit?"

Explain the statement, "When we get full of the Holy Spirit and we're praying in the Spirit, we are building back what the devil is trying to tear down."

What is meant by the scripture, "But ye, beloved, building up yourselves on your most holy faith, praying in the Holy Ghost (Jude 20).

Is it true that Satan secretly and gradually attacks our weakest points spiritually speaking? If so, name five ways he goes about it.

Give three reasons why spiritual boldness is critical to living a victorious Christian life.

STUDY QUESTIONS FOR BENEFIT FOUR: I WOULD THAT YE ALL SPAKE WITH TONGUES

What evidence do we have that the Holy Spirit is Pentecostal. (I Corinthians 14:5)

What is evidence that the Father is Pentecostal. (Isaiah 28:11, Joel 2:28-29)

Name the nine Gifts of the Spirit. (I Corinthians 12:8-12)

When trying to prove a doctrinal point in the Bible, why is it wrong to take a word or phrase out of context?

In I Corinthians 14:26 the scripture admonishes Spirit filled believers to "Let all things be done unto edifying." What does this mean? What are our responsibilities to God and each other?

In Matthew 6:24 and Revelation 3:15,16 the Word of God makes important statements about about the importance of "Spiritual Readiness." What is the responsibility of the believer? How can we know we are ready should God come or call us through death? What is the will of God relative to speaking in other tongues as the Spirit gives the utterance?

STUDY QUESTIONS FOR BENEFIT FIVE:
SPEAKING IN TONGUES OPENS OTHER DOORS

What is the difference between the gift of speaking in tongues and the gift of prophecy. (I Corinthians 14:1-6)

What is the Lord's plan for each of us in regard to the spiritual gifts?

Explain the statement, "you can always tell the difference between your prayer language and a normal message in tongues."

During the service Paul gives the order of the usage of the gifts of tongues and interpretation of tongues. (I Corinthians 14:27)

What is the order?

What is meant by the scripture in I Corinthians 14:28, "But if there be no interpreter, let him keep silence in the church and let him speak to himself, and to God." Should this occur in the service? What is the responsibility of the messenger in tongues? (vss. 28 & 33) What is meant by the statement, "when you go beyond two or three messages in tongues in one service, the messenger is in the flesh and not in the spirit."

Explain Paul's statement in 2 Timothy 1:6. "...stir up the gift of God which is in thee..."

STUDY QUESTIONS FOR BENEFIT SIX: NO SOUND WITHOUT MEANING

Explain I Corinthians 14:10, especially with reference to the phrase, "so many kinds of voices in the world, and none of them is without signification."

What is the common criticism by non spirit-filled believers in regards to "gibbering" when speaking in tongues, and how is that criticism answered?

What encouragements are given to whoever is seeking the baptism. Furthermore, what words of encouragement are given to those recently filled with the baptism and are tempted by the devil to doubt the experience is real.

Give the Greek meaning for the following words from Acts 2:4.
- a. Sound
- b. Wind
- c. Breath of God
- d. Rushing
- e. Mighty
- f. Loud noise

STUDY QUESTIONS FOR BENEFIT SEVEN: PRAYING AND SINGING WITH THE SPIRIT

What is meant by the statement, "we are 'true beings?'"

Which part of this triune being communicates directly to God?

What happens to our relationship with God when our spirit is overcome by the strong urges of our physical bodies?

Name the nine Fruits of the Spirit?

What is meant by the following statement, "The Holy Spirit is the speaking member of the Godhead."

Does it take more faith to receive the Baptism than it does to be saved? (Ephesians 2:8)

What is meant by I Corinthians 14:14, "For if I pray in an unknown tongue, my spirit prayeth."

Why can't you turn the Holy Spirit on and off in your mind as you would like?

Can the Holy Spirit dwell in an unclean temple?

What is the explanation for the statement, "There is a tremendous blessing to singing in the Spirit."

STUDY QUESTIONS FOR BENEFIT EIGHT: THIS IS THE REST

How does Isaiah 28:11-12 confirm, prove or validate the coming of the Baptism in the Holy Spirit (Acts 2:4), and give the assurance to believers that that same experience is very real and available to us today if we ask in faith believing.

In your opinion, why are there so many today who love Jesus and passionately preach and teach God's Holy Word, but yet will not accept the Baptism in the Holy Spirit with evidence of speaking in other tongues as the Spirit gives the utterance? (Acts 2:4)

Why is it so important that we as spirit-filled believers exemplify sound doctrine in the interpretation of God's Word as well as wisdom from above in preaching and teaching these truths.

In Isaiah 28:12 the words, "...this is the rest..." appears and carries a unique meaning. Give the meaning and summarize the explanation of this scripture.

The word "abide" includes in its meaning the phrase, "something that is permanent." Give two ways we can know that the Holy Spirit "abides" in our life.

In your own words, relate your understanding of the comparsion of the Holy Spirit's relationship.

CHAPTER SEVEN

The Nine Gifts of the Spirit

I want to look at the nine gifts of the Spirit listed in **I Corinthians 12:8-10 "For to one is given by the Spirit the word of wisdom; to another the word of knowledge by the same Spirit; To another faith by the same Spirit; to another the gifts of healing by the same Spirit; To another the working of miracles; to another prophecy; to another discerning of spirits; to another divers kinds of tongues; to another the interpretation of tongues".**

In order to understand the gifts of the Spirit, we must separate them from the gift of the Spirit. For the gifts to operate in the believer, that believer must first be saved and then be filled (baptized) with the Holy Spirit. Peter refers to that in **Acts 2:38 "…Repent, and be baptized every one of you in the name of Jesus Christ for the remission of sins, and ye shall receive the gift of the Holy Ghost".** This is the promise that if one repents and his sins are forgiven, he can receive the gift of the Holy Spirit. We know Peter is referring to the Baptism with the Holy Spirit, with the evidence of speaking in other tongues, as the Spirit gives the utterance, because of the context of the Scriptures, as he explains what has happened on the Day of Pentecost.

In the following verse, **Acts 2:39,** he refers to **"the promise",** that **"is unto you, and to your children, and to all that are afar off, even as many as the Lord our God shall call".** This is another direct statement concerning receiving the Baptism with the Holy Spirit. So, we know **"the gift"** refers to the individual receiving the Baptism with the Holy Spirit, so that the Holy Spirit can direct the **"gifts"**, "severally as he will". **1 Corinthians 12:11 "But all these worketh that one and the selfsame Spirit, dividing to every man severally as he will".**

Jesus refers to receiving the Holy Spirit as a gift in **Luke 11:13 "If ye then, being evil, know how to give good gifts unto your children: how much more shall your heavenly Father give the Holy Spirit to them that ask him"?** Again this is a direct reference to the gift of the Holy Spirit, and not a reference to the gifts of the Spirit.

The nine gifts of the Spirit describe the supernatural power that is imparted by the Holy Spirit for special ministries. The gifts are given for the edification of the church, in order that the church may be built and become what the Holy Spirit wants it to become. As you will see, when the gifts are operating in the church as the Spirit directs, the needs of people are going to be met and miracles will occur on a regular basis. That is God's plan for the church. But, He needs people through whom He can move and operate.

Paul states in **1 Corinthians 12:1 "Now concerning spiritual gifts, brethren, I would not have you ignorant".** He then states in **verse 4 "Now there are diversities of gifts, but the same Spirit".** The Holy Spirit has a variety of ministries. One of those ministries is giving gifts to believers.

The purpose of the gifts is given in **verse 7 "But the manifestation of the Spirit is given to every man to profit withal".** The word **"manifestation"** in the Greek is **"phanerosis"**, which means, **"making visible".** The visible manifestations would be the visible healings, miracles, prophecies, tongues, interpretations, words of wisdom and words of knowledge, and discernments of various kinds.

The nine gifts of the Spirit can be broken up into three different categories:

There are those that impart power to speak supernaturally:

1. **Prophecy**
2. **Tongues**
3. **Interpretation**

There are those that impart power to know supernaturally:

1. **The word of wisdom**
2. **The word of knowledge**
3. **Discernment**

There are those that impart power to act supernaturally:

1. **Faith**
2. **Miracles**
3. **Healings**

Therefore, these nine gifts are described as "the manifestation of the Spirit", "given to every man to profit withal". This is the Scriptural definition of the "manifestation" or the "making visible", of the Spirit: the operation of any of the nine gifts of the Spirit.

I want to look at the three gifts that "impart power to <u>speak</u> supernaturally".

The first gift is **Prophecy. Prophecy** is an utterance, which has been inspired by the Holy Spirit, revealing to the church, something that has been unknown beforehand, literally, foretelling the future. We are told in **1 Corinthians 14:39 "Wherefore, brethren, covet to prophesy, and forbid not to speak with tongues".** Here we are told to covet the gift of prophecy, and, forbid not those who speak with tongues.

This is not a gift you find only in the New Testament. You can see the gift of prophecy operating even in the Old Testament. You can read the prophecies of Isaiah, Jeremiah, Ezekiel and Daniel in the Old Testament and know that God used them in this area of ministry. These men were called by God and used by the Holy Spirit. **2 Peter 1:21 "For the prophecy came not in old time by the will of man: but holy men of God spake as they were moved by the Holy Ghost".** The prophecies were given by revelation, by the Holy Spirit. These men were filled with the Holy Spirit, but were not baptized with the Spirit. They did not speak with tongues, because that gift had not yet been given.

Isaiah prophesied in **Isaiah 28:11 "For with stammering lips and another tongue will he speak to this people",** that tongues would indeed be experienced by believers in the future.

Joel prophesied in **Joel 2:28,29 "And it shall come to pass afterward that I will pour out my spirit upon all flesh; and your sons and your daughters shall prophesy, your old men shall dream dreams, your young men shall see visions: And also upon the servants and upon the handmaids in those days will I pour out my spirit".**

Both Isaiah and Joel prophesied that tongues would come in the future, but tongues were not experienced in the Old Testament. The Holy Spirit, with this revelation, inspired both men.

I love the prophecy given in **Malachi 4: 2 "But unto you that fear my name shall the Sun of righteousness arise with healing in his wings..."** First of all, the word **"fear"** should have been translated **"love"** or **"revere"**. This prophecy is about Jesus. You can tell by looking at how **"Sun"** is spelled. The spelling is not "son", but "Sun", and it's capitalized, so, it has to refer to a person!

Malachi is saying that you, who love my name, referring to Jesus, the Sun of righteousness, shall **"arise"**. The word **"arise"** here in the Hebrew, means: **to irradiate, or shoot forth beams of light and power.**

From Malachi to the New Testament, there were 400 years of darkness referred to as the Dark Ages. The world was sitting in darkness, without light. Suddenly, Jesus comes and declares, **"...I am the light of the world..." John 8:12.** And, He began **"irradiating", "shooting forth beams of light and power"** across a darkened world!

When He comes, **He "arises", He "irradiates with beams of light and power",** with **"healing in his wings".** The word here for **"healing"** in the Hebrew means: **cure, medicine, deliverance, remedy, soundness and health**. Here is a prophecy that tells what Jesus would be like when He came! The prophecy is for those who love His name! Do you love Him?

Then the prophecy says He will have **"healing in his <u>wings</u>".** This does not refer to the wings of a building, because Jesus is not a building. This does not refer to the wings of a bird, because Jesus is not a bird. This does not refer to the wings of a plane, because Jesus is not a plane. The very word which is used here, and you can get set to be blessed, since it refers to a person, **refers to the border or the hem of His robe!**

There was a woman in **Luke 5:25-34,** who had an issue of blood, she had had for twelve years. The Word said she had suffered many things of many physicians, and had spent all that she had, and was nothing bettered, but rather grew worse. But, she heard Jesus was passing her way and she said in her heart, "If I may touch but his clothes, I shall be whole". She began pressing her way through the crowd to get to Jesus. It may have taken all her strength, but she reached out to touch the hem of His garment. I believe she wanted **the hem of His garment**. There would be **"healing in his wings".** When she touched Him, immediately, she was healed from her infirmity.

Here was a woman, who had access to the words of Malachi,

and writings concerning the Messiah Who was to come, **"But unto you that love my name shall the Sun of righteousness "irradiate with beams of light and power" with "cure, medicine, deliverance, remedy, soundness and health" in "the border of his robe". She said if I could just touch the hem of His garment that is what I will get!** And, she received exactly what she believed. She received her healing!

Malachi had been moved upon by the Holy Spirit to give a powerful prophecy, which came to pass when Jesus came. Prophecy is different from preaching. Preaching is generally the product of studying existing revelation, whereas prophecy is the result of spontaneous spiritual inspiration. Prophecy was never meant to take the place of preaching or teaching, but to supplement it with the inspirational touch.

There have been times in my own ministry, when I have been absolutely amazed at what the Lord would reveal to me. I remember one instance that stands out in my mind. I was preaching in a church where the pastor's son and daughter-in-law had lost a beautiful baby boy by Instant Crib Death. At the end of an altar service I felt impressed to have them come forward to pray for them. As I began praying, I felt impressed by the Holy Spirit to tell them they were going to have a new child, and that it would be a girl, which is what they had always wanted. The Lord gave them a beautiful baby girl.

That thought came from the Holy Spirit as a prophetic word. You can always tell if it comes from the Lord or not, **1 Thessalonians 5:19-21 "Quench not the Spirit. Despise not prophesying. Prove all things; hold fast that which is good".** You prove all things to see if they come to pass or not. You should always be concerned to see whether or not what you have said comes true. When the Holy Spirit is using the gift of prophecy, it will always come to pass. Paul told the church to test each message and to hold on to what is good and reject what appears to be unsound.

The purpose of the New Testament gift of prophecy is stated in **1 Corinthians 14:3 "But he that prophesieth speaketh unto men to edification, and exhortation, and comfort".** The words of the prophet are meant to bring edification to the church. The words are to help build the church. The words are to help instruct the church. The words are given to comfort the church.

Paul stated in **Romans 12:6 "Having then gifts differing according to the grace that is given to us, whether prophecy, let us prophesy according to the proportion of faith".** The gifts are given and exercised according to grace and the measure of faith, by the Holy Spirit, who divides to every man as He wills, according to **1 Corinthians 12:11.**

There are times in a service when a message in tongues may be given, followed by the interpretation, and then, a prophecy may be given. People may feel they sound alike. And, in reality they are a lot alike. **Tongues plus interpretation equals prophecy!** They are all given by inspiration of the Holy Spirit. They are three different gifts of the Spirit operating in the same service. The purpose of the gifts, again, is for the edification of the church. I will attempt to explain the difference in the following explanations of the gift of tongues and the interpretation of tongues.

The second gift that imparts power to speak supernaturally is the gift of tongues. It is referred to as "**...divers kinds of tongues...**" in **1 Corinthians 12:10.**

Acts 2:1-4 gives us the beginning of tongues in the New Testament. **Verse three states: "And there appeared unto them cloven tongues like as of fire, and it sat upon each of them".**

Along with this "**...sound from heaven as of a rushing mighty wind...**" came visible forked tongues like fire, sitting upon each one of the 120 gathered in the Upper Room. In that moment, they were both filled and baptized with the Holy Spirit, speaking in other tongues as the Spirit gave them utterance.

That which Isaiah had prophesied in **Isaiah 28:11** had come to pass. Those who had gathered in Jerusalem for the Feast of Pentecost, heard these 120 speaking in tongues, and **Acts 2:12** states **"And they were all amazed, and were in doubt, saying one to another, What meaneth this"?**

Peter had an explanation for their question. He said in **Acts 2:16-17 "But this is that which was spoken by the prophet Joel; And it shall come to pass in the last days, saith God, I will pour out of my Spirit upon all flesh…"** Here, we have the fulfillment of the prophecy of Joel, explaining what has happened.

The tongues referred to here is the initial evidence that they had been baptized with the Holy Spirit. One must receive this experience of tongues, in order to be used by the Holy Spirit in the usage of the gift of tongues.

The **"gift of tongues"** is the power of speaking supernaturally in a language never learned by the speaker. This is true for those receiving the Baptism of the Holy Spirit, speaking in their own prayer language, speaking to God. It is also true to those who speak in tongues, giving a message in tongues, with that message being interpreted, so the church can be edified.

You have praise addressed to God alone, as in **1 Corinthians 14:2 "For he that speaketh in an unknown tongue speaketh not unto men, but unto God…"**

And, you have a definite message for the church, as in **verse 5** of the same chapter, **"I would that ye all spake with tongues, but rather that ye prophesied: for greater is he that prophesieth than he that speaketh with tongues, except he inter-**

pret, that <u>the church may receive edifying</u>".

Speaking in tongues is done through immediate inspiration by
the Holy Spirit when one has received the gift. It can literally
become part of his make-up, mentally, so that he can exercise it
without direct inspiration. Paul stated that fact in **1 Corinthians
14:32 "And the spirits of the prophets are subject to the
prophets"**, and in **1 Corinthians 13:1 "Though I speak with
the tongues of men and of angels, and have not charity, I am
become as sounding brass, or a tinkling cymbal".**

I have been where people would give a message in tongues and
an interpretation would follow that was not inspired by the Holy
Spirit. I remember one church where the pastor's wife was
dying with cancer. There were messages in tongues and interpretations stating she would be healed. When she died there was
a great deal of confusion in the church. Some people even questioned God.

First of all, we are to try the Spirit to see if it is the Lord or not.
If it had been the Holy Spirit inspiring the people to speak, then
she would have been healed. It was evident that those who gave
the interpretation were speaking what the flesh wanted. They
wanted the pastor's wife to be healed. As a result, there was
confusion in the church. And, Paul stated in **1 Corinthians
14:33 "For God is not the author of confusion, but of peace,
as in all churches of the saints".**

This is why the exercise of vocal gifts of prophecy, tongues and
interpretation of tongues is commanded to be regulated and
judged as to whether it is under direct inspiration or whether the
person is exercising a gift of himself; **1 Corinthians 14:27-33.**

There have been times in our church services when a message in
tongues would be given, followed by an interpretation, when the
Lord would give exactly what the church needed during that
particular time. He knows what the church needs. He knows
how to supply those needs. When a message in tongues is given,

God is speaking to the church, through a yielded vessel, so the church may be edified. **Praise the Lord for the gift of tongues! Pray to be used by the Holy Spirit!**

The third gift that imparts power to speak supernaturally is the gift of interpretation of tongues.

The purpose of the gift of interpretation is to make known to the congregation, when a message has been given, the meaning of that message in the known language of the congregation. Usually the message is given in an unknown language to the congregation. Therefore,it has to be explained or translated, which is what an interpretation is.

When a message in tongues is given, followed by an interpretation, they are to be done by one individual at a time. Paul explains this in **1 Corinthians 14:27 "If any man speak in an unknown tongue, let it be by two, or at the most by three, and that by course; and let one interpret".**

The person giving the message is to speak loudly, commanding the attention of the church. The person giving the interpretation is to speak loudly, so that all can hear what the Lord is saying to the church.

I have been in services where people speak so softly when giving the message or interpretation that many cannot hear what is being said. When the Lord speaks to the church, **He wants everyone to hear what is being said.** The message is not only for a few standing or sitting close to the giver of the message in tongues and the interpretation of tongues, but for the entire body of believers. When one is being used by the Holy Spirit in the operation of any of the gifts of the Spirit, they should be aware of their responsibility to the entire body of believers. **Speak loudly enough for everyone to hear!**

The gift of interpretation of tongues is strictly a spiritual operation. The same Holy Spirit that inspired the message in tongues is also inspiring the interpretation of tongues. The interpretation of tongues is therefore inspirational and spontaneous.

I have been in services where the minister would be giving a prophetic word and someone would start giving a message in tongues, followed by the interpretation. In my opinion, that is totally out of order. The Holy Spirit is not going to stop the operation of one gift in order to have another gift operate. That is confusion, and the Lord is not the author of confusion.

There have been times when I have been preaching, and someone would start giving a message in tongues, that I have stopped them and told them they were out of order. Again, tongues will not interrupt prophecy. If the preaching of the Word is inspired, then the Holy Spirit will not inspire someone else to interrupt what He has already inspired.

I have had people tell me that they had felt quickened to give the message in tongues and who am I to tell them it wasn't from the Lord. Again, I have told them the Lord is not the author of confusion, **"And the spirits of the prophets are subject to the prophets", 1 Corinthians 14:32.**

It appears sometimes to be confusing in our church services. A message in tongues will be given, followed by the interpretation of tongues, and then a prophecy will be given. People ask, "Why would God give two gifts that end up virtually identical when used among the body in a church service? What is the difference between the gift of prophecy and the gift of tongues and interpretation of tongues when used in a public service"?

As we have seen in our study, tongues plus interpretation of tongues equals prophecy. The end result is the same. The gifts are for the edification of the church. The main difference between the gifts is stated in **1 Corinthians 14:22 "Wherefore tongues are for a sign, not to them that believe, but to them that believe not: but prophesying serveth not for them that believe not, but for them which believe".**

I have been in services when a message in tongues was given, followed by the interpretation, and people have run to the altar to give their hearts to the Lord. In one instance, the man who gave his heart to the Lord, said the Lord called him by name and told him, in his own language, He wanted him to serve Him. That man was an unbeliever, and tongues, plus interpretation of tongues, brought conviction to him, which in turn, brought edification to the church.

The gift of prophecy is given by the Holy Spirit to build up the assembled body of believers. When the prophecies come true, their faith is built. They trust the Lord more. They expect more, and as a result, receive more. This is the purpose of all the gifts: the edification of the church.

All three of the gifts that impart power to speak supernaturally are important. They are similar in their usage, and equally important in the church. Stir up the gift the Holy Spirit wants you to use!

I want to look now at the three gifts that "impart power to know supernaturally".

The first gift is **"The word of wisdom"**. The Holy Spirit gives to a believer, a supernatural revelation of how to deal with any problem that may arise. It is vitally important to know how to cope with things you may never have faced before. We run into those things many times in the ministry.

I remember several years ago when I was pastor at Faith Tabernacle in Oklahoma City, I had begun pushing the congregation in an attempt to get the new church built. I was facing a situation I had never faced before. In my eagerness to get the church built, instead of leading the congregation, I was pushing them. A shepherd leads the flock, he does not push them. I simply could not see what I was doing.

I had a wonderful friend, Dr. William Shell, who came to my office early one morning to share something with me he said the Lord had laid on his heart. He told me in the book of **James** there were two kinds of wisdom mentioned. Then he read to me the verses in **James 3:14-18 "But if ye have bitter envying and strife in your hearts, glory not, and lie not against the truth. This wisdom descendeth not from above, but is earthly, sensual, devilish. For where envying and strife is, there is confusion and every evil work. But the wisdom that is from above is first pure, then peaceable, gentle, and easy to be intreated, full of mercy and good fruits, without partiality, and without hypocrisy. And the fruit of righteousness is sown in peace of them that make peace"**.

Bill asked me what kind of wisdom had I been using in the church? Had I used earthly wisdom, which causes envy and strife, or had I been using the wisdom that is from above, which is pure, peaceable, gentle, and easy to be intreated? It was like I had been hit between the eyes with a baseball bat! I had not been using wisdom from above.

Webster's dictionary defines wisdom as "the capacity of judging soundly and dealing broadly with facts". I had not been judging soundly. I had not been dealing broadly with facts. I had ignored the fact I was pushing the congregation instead of leading them. I had made them uncomfortable and they were resisting what I was trying to get them to do. I had been preaching hard on faith in an effort to get them to believe God for more.

In fact, I had preached so much on faith, that in one of my board meetings, one of my best friends, Scott Taylor, stood to his feet, slapped his hand on the table, and walked out of the meeting saying, "faith, faith, that's all I hear. I get so tired of hearing about faith".

I thanked Dr. Shell for coming by and sharing with me what the Lord had impressed upon his heart. Then I picked up the phone and called my friend, Scott, who had walked out of our board meeting, and asked if he could come by the church to talk with me.

When Scott came, I told him what Dr. Shell had shared with me. Then I apologized to him for pushing him, and the church, instead of leading them. We embraced as the Holy Spirit began doing His work in our lives. I felt then that I knew what the Holy Spirit wanted me to do in our Sunday morning service.

The following Sunday morning, I stopped my message, and began sharing with the congregation, what had happened earlier that week, when Dr. Shell stopped to see me. I told the church I had called Scott and apologized to him, and that I wanted to apologize to them for pushing them instead of leading them.

I was not prepared for what happened next. People started standing all over the church and began apologizing to me for the things they had been saying about me. The Holy Spirit began healing feelings in that service that literally transformed Faith Tabernacle. And, from that morning on, Faith Tabernacle was never the same. The church worked together, pulled together, and began growing numerically, and, as that happened, the giving increased dramatically. The Lord knew what the church needed and the Holy Spirit began working in the lives of people who were obedient to Him. **Praise the Lord for the gift of wisdom!**

Joseph, in **Genesis 41,** was given wisdom from above. The Lord gave him the wisdom to interpret the dream Pharaoh had. Then the Lord gave Joseph the wisdom to tell Pharaoh what kind of a person was needed to handle the situation that was coming. Joseph received supernatural revelation from God.

In **Acts 6:3**, the apostles were speaking to the multitude of the disciples, whose numbers had grown in Jerusalem, and said, **"Wherefore, brethren, look ye out among you seven men of honest report, full of the Holy Ghost and wisdom, whom we may appoint over this business".**

The business, about which they referred, was the fact the widows had been neglected since they had all come together as believers. They had agreed together in **Acts 2:44-45,** that they would sell their possessions and goods, and give to every man as he had need.

The apostles said in **Acts 6:2 "...It is not reason that we should leave the word of God, and serve tables".** In other words, they did not feel they should have to attend to the tables where the collections were received and distributions to the people were being made. They said in **verse four, "But we will give ourselves continually to prayer, and to the ministry of the word".** They felt what was needed were men full of the Holy Spirit and wisdom to take care of the situation. That is still the need today in our churches. We need men, full of the Holy Spirit and wisdom, to handle the business of the church. What the apostles needed to do was to pray and prepare their hearts for ministry of the Word.

The Holy Spirit will give us wisdom in dealing with those outside the church. Paul said in **Colossians 4:5-6 "Walk in wisdom toward them that are without, redeeming the time. Let your speech be always with grace, seasoned with salt, that ye may know how ye ought to answer every man".**

It is vitally important that we know how to talk to unbelievers. Many times we turn people off when we attempt to talk to them about the Lord. Paul spoke of that in **1 Corinthians 2:4 "But the natural man receiveth not the things of the Spirit of God: for they are foolishness unto him: neither can he know them, because they are spiritually discerned".**

I have seen many, who possessed a lot of zeal, but not a lot of wisdom, cause people to leave church, and sadly, many of them never returned. As Spirit-filled believers, if we will yield ourselves to the Holy Spirit, He will give us the wisdom we need to reach the lost. We will know what to say and when to speak. We will not offend. We will not hurt someone's feelings. Our speech will always be with grace, seasoned with salt, coming from a heart of love.

We will be able, as Paul stated in **Colossians 1:27-28,** to preach **"...Christ in you, the hope of glory: ...warning every man, and teaching every man in all wisdom; that we may present every man perfect in Christ Jesus".**

May we, as James admonishes us in **James 1:5 "If any of you lack wisdom, let him ask of God, that giveth to all men liberally, and upbraided not; and it shall be given him",** ask the Lord to impart wisdom into our lives. **Wisdom is one gift we all need!**

The second gift that imparts power to <u>know</u> supernaturally is the word of knowledge!

The **"word of knowledge"** is supernaturally inspired utterance of facts spoken by one who has no previous knowledge of those facts. The knowledge comes from One who knows everything. Jesus said in **Matthew 10:26 "Fear them not therefore: for there is nothing covered, that shall not be revealed; and hid, that shall not be known".**

Webster defines knowledge as: "denotes acquaintance with, or clear perception of facts; enlightenment". The Lord knows everything there is to know about all of us, He is acquainted with all the facts, and those facts can be revealed by the Holy Spirit to anyone who yields himself or herself to Him.

I watched in amazement in 1971, in our fourteen-week revival at Faith Tabernacle in Oklahoma City, as the Holy Spirit used our evangelist in the usage of the gift of knowledge. People from our church would come forward for prayer for healing, and the evangelist would begin telling them what their need was, even before they could tell him. Miracle after miracle occurred. I knew he had no way of knowing their needs unless the Holy

Spirit revealed it to him. The gifts of the Spirit were operating, and the church was being blessed.

There is a real operation of the gifts and there is a counterfeit. The devil will always try to discredit what the Holy Spirit does by producing something that is not real. We have all read in the newspapers, and watched on T.V., the sad stories of evangelists who used microphones and hidden receivers to transmit information about individuals for whom they were going to pray. This was done in an effort to get people to believe they were being used in the operation of the gifts of the Spirit.

Peter had rebuked Simon in the eighth chapter of **Acts,** when Simon thought the gift of God could be purchased with money. Peter stated in **Acts 8:21 "Thou hast neither part nor lot in this matter: for <u>thy heart is not right in the sight of God</u>".** Men's hearts are not right with God when they try to use the gifts of the Spirit for profit or deception.

I remember on another occasion in Faith Tabernacle, when one of our families came out of church one Sunday morning to find their new car had been stolen. We called and reported the theft to the police and they began their investigation.

I began praying about the car being stolen and asked the Lord to help me find the car. While I was praying the next day, the Holy Spirit spoke to my heart and told me who had taken the car. The person I felt who had taken it was one of the young men in the church. I prayed diligently for quite a while because I didn't want the thought to be just my thought.

I picked up the phone and called the young man's house. Amazingly, he answered the phone. I called him by name and asked him where the car was. He said he didn't know what I was talking about. I told him the Holy Spirit had told me that he had taken the car and I wanted to know where the car was. He confessed he had taken the car and told me where it was. I told him I wanted him, and his parents, to come to the church and tell the people whose car he had taken, what he had done, and that he would get the car back. He came to the church with his parents and confessed what he had done and was able to get the car back for the people. The Holy Spirit was able to take care of the situation through the operation of the gift of the word of knowledge. The Holy Spirit had supernaturally revealed to me the facts, about which I had no way of knowing. As a result, the church was blessed, because the families were reconciled.

The difference between the word of wisdom and the word of knowledge is: that the word of wisdom gives the believer the wisdom needed to cope with any problem that might arise by using known facts, and the word of knowledge gives the revelation of unknown facts to the believer. Both gifts are to be desired. Pray for the Holy Spirit to use you!

The third gift that imparts power to <u>know</u> supernaturally is the gift of discerning of spirits.

The gift of discerning of spirits is supernatural revelation, which enables one to know if, what is happening is, of the Spirit, or of the flesh.

Webster defines discernment as: "mental quickness and accuracy in detecting or discriminating; keen insight". The Holy Spirit gives the believer that ability, to be immediately aware as to whether or not something is of God or not. We need that gift operating in our churches.

A number of years ago, Gretnia and I were preaching a revival in Enid, Oklahoma where we had been having a wonderful move of the Holy Spirit. As is the case, many times when that is happening, the devil will try to disrupt the meeting. While I was preaching Sunday morning, a man came into the church, carrying a large family Bible, and walked down to the front, and sat down. When I gave the invitation, he came forward, and supposedly gave his heart to the Lord. People had gathered around him, praying with him, when suddenly he began speaking in tongues.

When he began speaking, it was like cold chills ran down my spine. I turned to the pastor and told him that what the man was speaking was not of God. The pastor and the people did not believe what I said. They kept praying and talking to the man. It wasn't long until he told them he needed money to get to another destination. As it turned out, the pastor received phone calls from other pastors in the area, and the man had been in their churches, doing the same thing. The Holy Spirit, through the gift of discerning of spirits, had revealed to me what the man was doing.

Paul told Timothy in **1 Timothy 4:1 " Now the Spirit speaketh expressly, that in the latter times some shall depart from the faith, giving heed to seducing spirits, and doctrines of devils".** So, we know that there will be deception by the devil, as he attempts to seduce people by means of false preaching.

The Word states in **2 Timothy 4:3-4 "For the time will come when they will not endure sound doctrine; but after their own lusts shall they heap to themselves teachers, having itching ears; And they shall turn away their ears from the truth, and shall be turned unto fables".** We are living in that period of time now. People are attending churches where they can feel comfortable. They don't want to attend where they may feel guilt or conviction. The Gospel has been diluted and watered down because ministers do not want to offend anyone. Pastors, all too often, do not preach against sin. Pastors are catering to what people want, instead of doing what the Lord wants. As a result, many churches no longer have Sunday evening services, simply because pastors are afraid people won't come.

Where are our God-fearing, anointed, unafraid pastors? Where are God's men and women of faith and power, who are sensitive to the Holy Spirit? Where are those with the ability to discern what God wants, instead of doing what man wants? Only Spirit-filled ministers can discern what the Lord wants.

God's Word declares in **Hebrews 4:12 "For the word of God is quick, and powerful, and sharper than any two-edged sword, piercing even to the dividing asunder of soul and spirit, and of the joints and marrow, and is a discerner of the thoughts and intents of the heart"**. God's Word discerns our thoughts and knows the intents of our hearts. What do our hearts want? What are our thoughts? Are we doing what He wants, or, are we doing what our people want us to do?

We must pray, and cry, and fast, and seek the Lord, until we get full of the Holy Spirit. Then, He can speak to our hearts, and, if we desire to be used, He can give us the gift of discerning of spirits. When that happens, He will begin burning into our hearts, the desire to open the doors of our churches on Sunday evenings, so we can see the lost come to know the Lord.

I was called to preach a revival in Texas a few years ago. I had been to the church before, and we had had a wonderful move of the Holy Spirit. But, this time, we began the revival on Sunday morning, and the pastor announced that there would be no service that evening. Instead of having church, we went to different people's homes, where we ate and played games. No one was saved, and, no one was filled with the Holy Spirit.

Don't you know the devil is pleased with what is happening in many of our churches? He has us right where he wants us. We're no threat to him anymore. We're doing what he wants us to do, instead of what the Lord wants us to do.

We were born in the fire of Pentecost. Revivals lasted for weeks, as people were saved and filled with the Holy Spirit. The Lord was first in our lives. We wanted to please Him, because He was the most important thing in our lives. We knew what His will was. He wanted us meeting together, to worship Him. **That is still His will! Hebrews 10:25 "Not forsaking the assembling of ourselves together, as the manner of some is; but exhorting one another: and so much the more, as ye see the day approaching"**.

Many churches have stopped having revivals. The role of the evangelist is being diminished. Churches are too busy anymore to take time for revivals. We have time for softball and basketball practices and games, but don't have time for revival. We have time for social activities for all ages, but we don't have time for revival. Revival services have been reduced to Sunday services only. In some instances, services will go, maybe Sunday through Wednesday.

While traveling as an evangelist, there have been times when the Holy Spirit would be moving, and I thought surely the pastor would go on with the revival, but he would inform me they had a ball game scheduled the next night, and it wouldn't be possible to go on.

It doesn't take much of the Spirit to be able to discern what the Lord would want. He is more interested in souls being saved and believers being filled with the Holy Spirit, than He is about satisfying the flesh of man. Too many of our churches have become social clubs, more interested in pleasing man, than pleasing God.

We must once again, begin seeking for the fullness of the Holy Spirit, so we may be used in the operation of the gift of discerning of spirits! May we ever be sensitive to the Holy Spirit, to know what He wants!

There are three gifts that enable us to act supernaturally.

The first gift that enables us to <u>act</u> supernaturally is the gift of faith!

The gift of faith is a special faith, given to an individual to believe God for miraculous things. It comes from a special enduement of power, by the Holy Spirit, to Spirit-filled believers. The gift of faith will change your life. You will begin believing that the impossible will become possible.

Hebrews 11:6 states, **"But without faith it is impossible to please him: for he that cometh to God must believe that he is, and that he is a rewarder of them that diligently seek him"**. God's Word says we cannot please Him without faith. We must have faith to believe that Jesus is the Son of God, to believe that He hears and answers our prayers, to believe He can forgive our sins.

There must come a time when we know, that we know, that we know, who He is and what He can do. God has dealt to every man a measure of faith, according to **Romans 12:3 "For I say, through the grace given unto me, to every man that is among you, not to think of himself more highly than he ought to think; but to think soberly, according as God hath dealt to every man the measure of faith"**.

If we want the faith that God has given us to grow, we must begin building our faith, through the reading, studying, and hearing of God's Word. **Romans 10:17 "So then faith cometh by hearing, and hearing by the word of God"**. The Lord has given us the means to increase our faith. It is up to us to do it.

Paul tells us in **Romans 12:6 "Having then gifts differing according to the grace that is given to us..."** The nine gifts of the Spirit in **1 Corinthians 12** are given according to the unmerited grace we have received, and the measure of our faith. If we want more of the gifts operating in our lives, we must have faith enough to believe for them.

How much faith do you have?

Do you have enough faith to believe for your salvation?
Do you have enough faith to believe for the gift of faith to operate in your life?
Do you have enough faith to believe for any of the other gifts of the Spirit to operate in your life?
Are you satisfied with the level of faith you possess?

I have often thought, if I just had the gift of faith operating in my life, I could believe the Holy Spirit for all the other gifts. The gift of faith is a special quality of faith. The amount of faith you possess all depends on where you are in your "faith walk".

Two times in my ministry, as we were preparing to enter into a building program, I fell on my face, seeking the perfect will of God. In each instance, I stayed on my face until I had that assurance that the Lord would be with us, and bring us through victoriously. The Lord gave me that special gift of faith to believe that everything would be all right, and that all our needs would be met.

I have to admit that there were times when my faith was tested to the limit. But, each time, I would fall on my knees, and on my face, before the Lord, reminding Him that He had promised to see us through. Each time, He would answer my prayers, and we saw the completion of the building projects.

When the Lord answers your prayers and supplies your need, it is easier to believe He will do the same thing the next time you call upon Him. You read His Word, and see the many times He answered prayers and supplied needs, and you know He is no respecter of persons, so it builds your faith to believe Him for greater things.

Hebrews 11:1 states, "Now faith is the substance of things hoped for, the evidence of things not seen". I like to think in terms of **"now faith".** We can believe the Lord, **"now".** We don't have to wait until sometime later to believe. He is the God of our generation, **"now",** just as He has been the God of every generation.

I love the **11th chapter of Hebrews.** It is a declaration of the power of faith.
Verse 3 "Through faith we understand that the worlds were framed by the word of God."

Verse 4 "By faith Abel offered unto God a more excellent sacrifice than Cain, by which he obtained witness that he was righteous..."

Verse 5 "<u>By faith</u> Enoch was translated that he should not see death; and was not found, because God had translated him..."

Verse 7 "<u>By faith</u> Noah, being warned of God of things not seen as yet, moved with fear, prepared an ark to the saving of his house..."

Verse 8 "<u>By faith</u> Abraham, when he was called to go out into a place which he should after receive for an inheritance, obeyed; and he went out, not knowing whither he went".

Verse 11 "<u>Through faith</u> also Sara herself received strength to conceive seed, and was delivered of a child when she was past age..."

Verse 20 "<u>By faith</u> Isaac blessed Jacob and Esau concerning things to come".

Verse 24 "<u>By faith</u> Moses, when he was come to years, refused to be called the son of Pharaoh's daughter".

Verse 27 "<u>By faith</u> he forsook Egypt, not fearing the wrath of the king..."

Verse 28 "<u>Through faith</u> he kept the Passover, and the sprinkling of blood, lest he that destroyed the firstborn should touch them".

Verse 29 "<u>By faith</u> they passed through the Red Sea as by dry land..."

Verse 30 "<u>By faith</u> the walls of Jericho fell down, after they were compassed about seven days".
Verse 31 "<u>By faith</u> the harlot Rahab perished not with them that believed not, when she had received the spies with peace".

The gift of faith, operating in our lives, will produce miracles, just as it did through all of these in God's Word. They all received that special faith, where they were lifted out of the realm of natural and ordinary faith, into supernatural faith, to believe they could triumph over anything they might face.

That same kind of faith is available to us today through the gift of faith operating in our lives!
\
The second gift that imparts power to <u>act</u> supernaturally is the gift of healing!

The gift of healing is the supernatural ability, given by the Holy Spirit, to a believer to minister health to the sick, through prayer. It is very similar to the gift of working of miracles. The main difference between the two gifts is that the gift of healing can be progressive in its operation, while the gift of working of miracles is instantaneous in its results.

A perfect example of the gift of healing is seen in **Mark 8:22-25 "And he cometh to Bethsaida; and they bring a blind man unto him, and besought him to touch him. And he took the blind man by the hand, and led him out of the town; and when he had spit on his eyes, and put his hands upon him, he asked him if he saw ought. And he looked up, and said, I see men as trees, walking. After that he put his hands again upon his eyes, and made him look up: and he was restored, and saw every man clearly"**. The man was healed, but Jesus prayed for him twice. It was progressive healing.

Several years ago, when I was pastor at Faith Tabernacle in Oklahoma City, I received a phone call from a close friend of mine, with whom I had gone to school. He was at St. Anthony hospital, where his wife had been brought after attempting suicide. He asked if I could come and pray for her. He told me she was on life-support, and was not expected to live.

When I arrived at the hospital, they took me into the intensive care unit, where she had been placed. I went to her bedside and began talking to her. I told her I was sure she could hear me and there were things I wanted her to know. I told her; first of all, the Lord loved her. Then I told her He wanted to forgive her of her sins, and, that He wanted to heal her.

I asked her to pray the sinner's prayer with me, and then I asked the Lord to touch her and heal her body. We could not see any indication of a response from her at that moment. I visited with her husband and told him we would be praying for her, and my wife and I left.

Shortly after we left, my friend told me they began to see movement from his wife. It was not long afterwards; she regained consciousness, and began talking.

Just a few days later, she was dismissed from the hospital, and came to the church, where she gave a thrilling testimony. She shared how she had heard my voice when I began talking to her in the hospital. She told the church she had prayed the sinner's prayer when I had prayed with her. She said there was a sweet peace, which swept over her at that moment, and she felt everything was going to be all right. Then she said, " I stand before you today, healed in body and soul". The gift of healing had operated and she was healed and saved.

We have seen over the years, many who have been used by the Holy Spirit, in the operation of the gift of healing. When healings occur, people will come to see what the Lord is doing. Many have been healed through the ministry of men like Smith Wigglesworth, Jack Coe, Oral Roberts, as well as many others.

As we have seen, not everyone is healed in his or her services, or in our church services. People are not healed because we want them to be healed. They are healed when the Lord touches them. Allowances must be made for the sovereignty of God, and the sick person's attitude and spiritual condition.

Jesus said in **Luke 4:27 "And many lepers were in Israel in** the time of Eliseus the prophet; and none of them was cleansed, saving Naaman the Syrian". So, not all the lepers were healed. We can't always understand the way the Lord operates. I only know that He has a plan, and He is working out His plan in our best interest.

There were times when even Christ was limited in His miracle working ability. **Matthew 13:58 "And he did not many mighty works there because of their unbelief".** Unbelief by one person can hinder the operation of miracles, even though another individual may possess the gifts of the Spirit.

As believers, we should pray for the sick. Jesus said in **Mark 16:18 "...they shall lay hands on the sick, and they shall recover".**

James 5: 14 "Is any sick among you? Let him call for the elders of the church; and let them pray over him, anointing him with oil in the name of the Lord". The "elders" in the early church were the ministers and the deacons. The word "elders" in the Greek is "presbuteros". It is also used of older men and women.

May we begin hungering and thirsting after the things of the Spirit. If we will, there is no telling what the Lord may do in our lives.

The last gift that imparts power to <u>act</u> supernaturally is the gift of the working of miracles!

The gift of the working of miracles is literally the working of power, God's power, manifested through man. The gift of miracles can literally intervene in the ordinary course of nature. It can counteract natural laws, if necessary. It can produce things that are thought to be impossible.

The Lord has intended for the church to be filled with power. He said in **Acts 1:8 "But ye shall receive power, <u>after that the Holy Ghost is come upon you</u>..."** When you receive the

Baptism with the Holy Spirit, you have received the giver of the gifts. Every believer can have the gifts operating in their lives, if they get full enough of the Holy Spirit, and will yield himself or herself to Him.

I have been asked, "Can one person possess all the gifts"? The answer is yes. Paul had all the gifts operating in his life. There have been times in my own life when all the gifts have operated. It is very humbling to feel you have been used by the Holy Spirit in the operation of any of the gifts.

I was preaching a revival in Mt. Morris, Michigan a few years ago, when in one of our services; several deaf mutes came forward to seek for the Baptism of the Holy Spirit. I began praying for them through their interpreter, and gave instructions on how to receive the Baptism. In just a few minutes, suddenly, they began speaking in tongues, as the Holy Spirit gave them the utterance. Needless to say, there was tremendous rejoicing, as the church heard them speaking in tongues. The deaf mutes had never spoken before that glorious experience, but the Lord gave them a heavenly language to speak. They were speaking to God. It was a marvelous miracle, which caused many people to come and see what the Lord was doing in the revival.

I was in revival in Miami, Florida several years ago, when a lady, forty-two years of age, began attending the services. She came forward night after night to receive prayer for healing of her blindness. She told us later that she had been blind all of her life. Night after night, I prayed for her to be healed, but nothing happened. The revival continued an extra week, and she kept coming forward for prayer every night.

I'll never forget it as long as I live, but the last night, after almost everyone had left, she came forward and asked if I would pray for her one more time. I reached out and laid my hands upon her again, and asked the Lord to touch and heal her eyes, just as I had done every other night. But, this time, something happened! She began crying, "I can see! I can see!" Instantly, the Lord gave her sight. We had the most wonderful time of rejoicing, as she cried and cried, looking around to see people she had never seen before. It was a miracle from the Lord. It had not mattered how many times we had prayed before, He touched her in His own time.

I believe that all the other services had served to build her faith, so she could believe the Lord for her miracle that night. Miracles will get people's attention.

Look at the many miracles in the life of Moses!

His rod was turned into a serpent, and then, the serpent into a rod again.
His hand turned leprous, and then his hand was healed of leprosy. These were done to get the attention of the Children of Israel.

The miracles of the ten plagues were done to get Pharoah's attention.

Look at the miracles in the life of Jesus!

John 2:11 "This beginning of miracles did Jesus in Cana of Galilee, and manifested forth his glory: and his disciples believed on him".

Jesus performed miracles to demonstrate that He was, Who He said He was! The purpose of all miracles of God is to manifest His glory.

Does God get more glory out of the weakness, helplessness, defeat, sin, sickness and failure of His children or out of their power, victories, holiness, health and success? Which then is the will of God?

Jesus healed the man sick of the palsy in Mark 2:1-12.
Jesus healed the man with the withered hand in Mark 3:1-5.
Jesus stilled the storm in Mark 4:35-41.

**Jesus healed the demoniac of Gadara in Mark 5:1-20.
Jesus healed the woman with the issue of blood in Mark
5:25-34**.

These are just a few of the many miracles Jesus did while here
on earth. There were miracles of healing, and miracles of changing weather conditions and calming troubled waters.

Again, miracles are works of power, that men might know the
power of God!

The shadow of Peter produced miracles in **Acts 5:15
"Insomuch that they brought forth the sick into the streets,
and laid them on beds and couches, that at the least the
shadow of Peter passing by might overshadow some of
them"**. Just imagine, if you will, people lined up on the streets
of Jerusalem, on beds and couches, as Peter passes by. As his
shadow falls upon them, suddenly, they begin jumping to their
feet, healed by the power of God! It didn't matter what their
infirmity may have been. **Verse 16 stated, "...bringing sick
folks, and them vexed with unclean spirits: and they were
healed every one".** That is the kind of power that is available to
anyone, through whom the gift of miracles can operate.

You can see that power evident in the lives of the apostles in
**Acts 5:12-14 "And by the hands of the apostles were many
signs and wonders wrought among the people; and they
were all with one accord in Solomon's porch. (See the
importance of being of one mind and one accord). And of
the rest durst no man join himself to them: but the people
magnified them. And believers were the more added to the
Lord, multitudes both of men and women"**.

You may say, "But, those were the apostles, and we don't have
the same power they had". I beg to differ with you! Peter stated
in **Acts 10:34 "Then Peter opened his mouth, and said, Of a
truth I perceive that God is no respecter of person"**. There
are miracles happening today, all over the world, through Spirit-

filled believers. Our missionaries share miracle after miracle they experience on their fields of labor. Those miracles enable them to reach the lost.

Gretnia and I experienced the miracle working power of God early in our ministry. We had come in from church on the weekend, and had used all the gasoline in our car. The gas gage showed completely empty. The car was a 1956 Chevrolet, which had been given to Gretnia by her dad, Tommy Grant. Gretnia was in school, and I worked downtown in Oklahoma City. She had to go to school, which was quite a distance from where we lived, and I had to go to work after I took her to school, so it involved a lot of driving.

We knelt down and prayed before we went to bed, and asked the Lord to perform a miracle and to provide gasoline for the car, or money for gasoline, at least until I got paid on the following Friday. We went out the next morning and turned on the ignition, and to our amazement, the gas gage was up to over half a tank. That was enough gasoline for the week! Paul stated in **Philippians 4:19 "But my God shall supply all your need according to his riches in glory by Christ Jesus"**.

There may be some who would say," Your families put gasoline in your car without you knowing about it". That could have been true, if they had known about it, but no one knew that we were out of gasoline! No one knew, except the Lord! I have shared that testimony as we have traveled all over the country.

I have watched the Lord supply our needs, miraculously, many times. It has built our faith. We know that if we are obedient to Him, He will supply all our needs.

I remember on another occasion, we were in a missionary service, and the Lord spoke to me to give the last five dollars we had, in the offering that night. I tried to reason with the Lord, and told him that I was going to use that money to put gasoline in the car to get home. We were pastors in another town and had to drive home that night. But, the Lord told me again to put the money in the offering. I put the money in the offering, and we made it home that night without any trouble. The next morning, before 7 A.M., we had a knock at the door. There stood a man from Oklahoma City, who had driven almost thirty miles to get to our house, and told me the Lord had awakened him early that morning and told him to bring us an offering. The Lord gave us far more than we had put in the offering the night before. **"...My God shall supply all your need ..."**

Acts 19:11-12 "And God wrought special miracles by the hand of Paul: So that from his body were brought unto the sick handkerchiefs or aprons, and the diseases departed from them, and the evil spirits went out of them". Imagine, from his body, handkerchiefs and aprons were taken, and placed on the bodies of those who had need of healing, or who needed deliverance, and they were healed and delivered. Special miracles were done.

Many times, in our worship services, I have anointed a cloth, so it could be taken and placed on the body of someone who was sick. And, as you can see, from **Acts 19: 11,12 "And God wrought special miracles by the hands of Paul: So that from his body were brought unto the sick handkerchiefs or aprons, and the diseases departed from them, and the evil spirits went out of them",** that that is perfectly Scriptural. The Lord has many ways to perform miracles.

Miracles should be a part of every worship service. We serve a miracle-working Lord, and He is in our midst every time we gather together to worship Him. Pray and ask the Holy Spirit to give you the gift of the working of miracles!

STUDY QUESTIONS FOR CHAPTER FOURTEEN

Explain the difference between the gift of tongues and the gifts of the Spirit. What must one experience in order to receive the gifts of the Spirit?

For what purpose are the nine gifts of the Spirit given?

What does the word "manifestation" mean in the Greek, and what would be classified as "manifestations"?

Into what three categories can the gifts be divided and how are they different?

What are the three gifts that impart power to speak supernaturally?

How would you describe the gift of prophecy? Is it only seen operating in the New Testament? If not, where else does it operate and give examples?

How is prophecy received and by whom is its given?

What does the word "arise" mean in the prophecy given by the prophet Malachi?

What does the word "healing" mean in Malachi 4:2? Who can receive "healing"?

What does the term "in his wings" mean? Who in the New Testament received the fulfillment of that prophecy?

Explain the difference between prophecy and preaching.

How can you tell if a prophecy is true or not and give Scripture to confirm your answer?
What is the purpose of the gift of prophecy?

_____ plus _____ equals prophecy?

What is the gift of tongues and to whom is it addressed? How does this differ from one's prayer language?

Can one speak in tongues without inspiration of the Holy Spirit? Give Scripture to verify your answer.

How can a message in tongues and the interpretation of tongues bring confusion to a church?

What is the purpose of the gift of interpretation?

What Scripture regulates how many messages in tongues and interpretation of tongues that should be given in any one service? How many can be given?

What is the purpose of speaking loudly when giving a message in tongues or an interpretation of tongues?

Why would the Holy Spirit not interrupt one gift so that another gift could operate?

What is the difference between the gift of prophecy and the gift of tongues plus interpretation of tongues?

Name the three gifts that impart power to know supernaturally.

Define the gift of the word of wisdom.

What two kinds of wisdom are mentioned in the book of James?

How does Webster define wisdom?

Name at least one Old Testament character who received wisdom from above.

What was the "business" referred to in Acts 6:3?

How can we receive the wisdom we need in dealing with those outside the church? Cite the Scriptures.

What is the gift of the word of knowledge and from whom does it come?

What is the purpose of the devil producing a counterfeit of the gifts of the Spirit?

What is the difference between the word of wisdom and the word of knowledge?

Describe the gift of discerning of spirits.

How can the gift of discerning of spirits help in our church services?

How does the devil attempt to seduce people? Cite Scripture.

How is the Lord able to discern our thoughts and what is in our heart?

What is God's will concerning our meeting together to worship Him in Hebrews 10:25?

What have many of our churches become?

Name the three gifts that enable us to act supernaturally.

Explain the gift of faith.

What is the purpose of the "measure of faith" in Romans 12:3?

What causes our faith to grow?

What must we do if we want more of the gifts operating in our lives?

The gift of faith is a _____ _____ of faith. It depends on where you are in your "_____ _____".

Explain the gift of healing.

What is the main difference between the gift of healing and the gift of working of miracles?

When are people healed?

Why were there times when the Lord was limited in His miracle-working ability?

Are we to pray for the sick? What are we to do when someone is sick?

Define the gift of the working of miracles.

Can one person possess all the gifts of the Spirit? If so, who?

What were some of the miracles in the life of Moses?

\What is the purpose of all miracles?

How can we have the same power to produce miracles as the apostles had?

Is it Scriptural to anoint a cloth to be placed on someone? What Scripture proves that?

CONCLUSION

I have attempted in these few chapters to create a desire in people's hearts to explore what the Bible has to say about "What is Pentecost Really Like", and what "The Benefits of Speaking in Other Tongues" are to the believer. I have tried to explain in my own words what the Nine Gifts of the Spirit are. Paul spoke to Timothy in **2 Timothy 2:15 "Study to shew thyself approved unto God, a workman that needeth not to be ashamed, rightly dividing the word of truth".**

It is essential we know what God's Word has to say about these subjects. There is much in the Old Testament and New Testament as well, about the subjects, as I have endeavored to show you in this book. If the Bible makes much of something, then we need to make much about it as well. You will never know for sure about speaking in tongues or what the gifts of the Spirit are until you have searched the Scriptures for yourselves.

There have been a number of times in my revivals when people from other denominations, who did not believe in speaking in tongues, would come forward to seek for the Holy Spirit. When I began praying for them, I would ask, "What do you want the Lord to do for you"? They would say, "I want everything the Lord has for me". Then I would tell them to tell the Lord, if He had anything more for them than what they had received up until that time, to give it to them. I have been thrilled many times as I have seen those hungry hearts filled with the Holy Spirit, speaking in tongues.

I was in revival in McAlester, Oklahoma several years ago when eight young people from a local church visited the revival one night. The church they attended did not believe in speaking in tongues. The young people from First Assembly had invited them to the revival. The Holy Spirit was moving in a mighty way when I asked, "How many are ashamed of the Lord"? No one raised his or her hand. Then I said, "If you're not ashamed of the Lord, then I want you to join us in an old-fashion Jericho march"! You could hear the gasp of the people!

Those eight young people stepped out and joined the Jericho march. They weren't ashamed of the Lord. About halfway around, they came to the altar, where they stopped. They were weeping as the Holy Spirit touched their hearts. I asked them what they wanted from the Lord. In unison, they cried, "everything the Lord has us". In just a few moments, all eight were speaking in tongues, as they were filled with the Holy Spirit.

The Lord is waiting for hungry hearts to come to Him. Jesus said in **Matthew 5:6 "Blessed are they which do hunger and thirst after righteousness: for they shall be filled"**. He longs to fill you.

I pray we have a renewed interest in the Holy Spirit in our churches. I pray we have a new desire for the gifts to operate in our lives. I pray we begin placing an emphasis in our preaching on the subjects of the Baptism and the gifts of the Spirit. I pray for a sovereign move of the Holy Spirit. I pray we come to the realization of the power available to us through receiving the Holy Spirit. I pray we all are filled, speaking in other tongues, being used by the Holy Spirit in the operation of the nine gifts, utilizing the benefits the Lord has made available to us.